RECOGNITION TO RECOVERY:
HOW TO LEAVE YOUR ABUSIVE EX BEHIND FOR GOOD!

BY CARON KIPPING

Facts about domestic abuse

Domestic abuse happens to 1 in every 4 women, 1 in every 6 men and 1 in 5 children.

2 women die every week in the UK as a direct result of domestic abuse.

On average people live with domestic abuse for 2-3 years before they get help.

Health conditions associated with abuse include: asthma, bladder and kidney infections, cardiovascular disease, fibromyalgia, chronic pain syndromes, central nervous system disorders, gastrointestinal disorders, migraines/headaches.

Domestic abuse often leaves victims with reproductive consequences too, including gynaecological disorders, sexually transmitted infections, pre-term difficulties and pregnancy difficulties.

At least a fifth (18%) of children in domestic abuse households are injured as a result of the abuse.

Domestic abuse has significant psychological consequences for victims, including anxiety, depression, suicidal behaviour, low self-esteem, inability to trust others, flashbacks, sleep disturbances and emotional detachment.

Domestic abuse victims are at risk of post-traumatic stress disorder (PTSD).

Nearly one in three women who suffer from domestic abuse during their lifetime report that the first incidence of violence happened while they were pregnant.

Domestic violence is higher amongst those who have separated, followed by those who are divorced or single.

Each year there are over 1 million calls to police in England and Wales about domestic abuse, and on average someone contacts the police every 30 seconds for help with domestic abuse.

All statistics from Safe Lives Organisation 2020.

Testimonials for Recognition to Recovery

Claire Batchelor: Advocacy Manager at The Dash Charity:

I have worked with Caron for many years through our careers in midwifery and Domestic Abuse.

Caron has achieved accredited qualifications and has supported individuals through their journeys as well as training professionals to a high level on signs of domestic abuse and resources available. Caron is passionate about her work and will always go above and beyond to support anyone experiencing domestic abuse.

Through her personal and professional experience, Caron has written the book for anyone experiencing domestic abuse.

Caron is family oriented and wants individuals to know that there is always support available to end domestic abuse and this book can educate and empower individuals to make informed choices.

Well done Caron ... Domestic abuse should be talked about and not hidden It should be seen and heard!!!

Rosie C:

What a great read. It was brilliant and a real insight into what goes on and how to overcome it. I think it will be useful to past/present victims as well as friends and families who want to have an understanding in order to offer help and support!

Great job!

Louise Barnes Hypnotherapy

This book is just what is needed right now! This book will help individuals, their family or friends and professionals identify domestic abuse, the tactics used and more, you'll be surprised! The practical, factual, step by step approach makes it easy to follow. Caron uses all her personal experience, expertise and knowledge to give you the tools and information that you need to take back control of your life.

In my experience of working with those who struggle with mental health/domestic abuse this book will help the reader feel less isolated, give them practical strategies to help them stay strong, cope better and learn how to manage anxiety, worry and life's ups and downs.

Small steps lead to greater achievements and life is too short for regrets, so take the first step.........get this book! Yes, it's your life so live it as you want to! This book will help you do it.

Dee

I wish that I had access to a book like this ten years ago when I started my journey to leave my controlling & abusive husband who I had been married to for 15 years. He was a City Lawyer and I was a Marketing Professional and became a stay- at -home mum to bring up our daughter.

I started my journey to leave him when my daughter was 8 years old. It took 6 years of intense and protracted litigation, Child Act proceedings, Non-Molestation and Restraining

Orders to protect myself and our daughter from him, as well as financial proceedings to get my freedom.

My daughter is now 18 years old, and has a bright future ahead of her. I have a fulfilling job and am currently considering retraining and love the idea of being a part-time student whilst working. I am in a healthy happy relationship with my partner and getting married in 2021.

My ex-partner no longer lives rent free in my head!

Caron helped and supported me and gave me the strength and belief to deal with all these battles I have had to overcome, to navigate my way through the rigid processes that exist both the legal world and, dealing with Authorities such as Social Services. Throughout, her support helped me deal with the consistent abuse of court proceedings and mental abuse from my ex-husband and this book can help you too.

It becomes complicated when you are putting orders in place to protect yourself from an abusive partner, but you are expected by the Courts, Social Services, school to co-parent with this abusive person. How can this work? Caron helped me develop strategies to stay in control and be prepared, which made me realise that I could steer things in the right direction for the right outcome.

What became clear was that understanding these processes & procedures ensured that I remained calm and in control of as much of my life as possible. At times getting to the finishing line seemed impossible to me, but I visualised a life of being "normal" - not being scared anymore, smiling and laughing again and being independent in all areas of my life. I wanted my daughter to have a good role model of what it's like to live life your own way and have dreams and opportunities again.

For anyone going through the trauma of abuse from their partner, this book really can help support you and help you realise that you can make that decision to make things different. You can, once again be in control, and this is your life! What does that life look like for you?

Alex

I found Caron just at the right time, I had already left my emotionally abusive partner and assumed it would end there but the abuse, manipulation and control escalated; using the children, our finances and threatening to 'expose' me as someone who had stolen from him and was an unfit parent. I was feeling desperate and despondent, surely leaving would have fixed this? When I contacted Caron, she immediately recognised what I was going through, she gave me some great advice and some really simple things I could do to get my life back under my control; things that my friends couldn't always help with as they were too mad with him and didn't feel equipped. Things like boundaries, knowing what and when to respond to his messages, self- care and really focussing on what is important. I am now out of the other end and whilst it is still tough at times; Caron was right, it will stop and she helped me get myself through it; Stronger!

Molly

Anyone who is in or has been in a controlling relationship should read this! This book is amazing, I am so proud of you!

Katie

Working with Caron has been an absolute revelation! I have learnt things about my past relationships that I didn't know, such as I was in an abusive relationship for ten years but didn't realise!

Her kind, patient and understanding nature has gently guided me through her programme and I have learnt so much from her. I have been able to understand my past relationships as well as understanding what I want from future relationships.

I would highly recommend Caron's coaching. She provided valuable insight with her experience and knowledge whilst allowing you to have lightbulb moments of your own.

Alison March – Founder of www.thegrouphug.com

I have known Caron for a couple of years now and have always found her to be easy going, positive and a very strong and determined woman. Her strength is infectious and even though I have not had any formal coaching with her, even chatting to her has made a real difference to my life with the regards to the domestic, economic and post separation abuse I have endured.

Caron's book is a must-read for anyone who is going through domestic abuse or who has been a past victim of it, whether physical or emotional or both. As I read her book, I felt as though Caron was in the room with me as it is written as Caron speaks. Many self-help books are too intense and use technical terminology; this book delivers its message in simple, plain English and is perfect.

As a victim of Domestic Abuse, I know that your mind can be overwhelmed with thoughts and emotions and Caron completely understands this. I have heard great things about her from The Group Hug community. She is an empathic person who encourages change and new beginnings. This book demonstrates that there is a new life to be had and Caron is on hand to help you to move from simply existing to seeing that there is a bright new future ahead of you if you want it. So don't delay, I did it, Caron did it and so can you!

Kelly

Very informative and hard hitting. Reassuring to know I am not alone and I'm certainly not going mad! Thank you for taking your experience and turning it into a positive to help others. So much focus is required in this space. Awareness is survival as is the support from people like yourself.

Delia Donovan, CEO, Domestic Violence New South Wales

Caron's 14 years working in the domestic abuse field as well as surviving terrible domestic abuse herself provides for an exceptional insight into lived experience and some of the service frameworks readers may require.

This book provides practical advice, guidance and tips for anyone thinking about leaving an abusive partner as well as guiding those wanting to learn about domestic abuse and others who may be on the initial road to self-discovery.

The knowledge, expertise and passion provided by Caron jumps out of the pages and means you will feel supported as you read the text!

The information in the book is also helpful for anyone wanting to learn about the signs, symptoms, myths and risk indicators of domestic abuse.

Recognition to Recovery provides a systematic account that anyone in the community can pick up. I love the bite size chunks of advice that are easily digestible.

This book will support you, guide you and provide you with hope! You are not alone.

Foreword:

I would not have reached this point in my life where I thought it would even be possible to write a book without the help of my family and friends who were there for me.

Whatever you did for me, big or small, please know I have never forgotten. Without your help I would never have got out. I would never have found out what I was capable of achieving. I will always be truly grateful.

Contents

CHAPTER 5:

Introduction

This book is for anyone considering leaving their controlling partner, and for those who have already left, but who might still be struggling. You may be a friend or a family member reading this book on behalf of someone else, ready to pass on the tips and tricks to them as and when they need them.

You can dip in and out of this book – you can re-read chapters and you can try these techniques more than once, if they don't work, don't give up - keep going. Try them again – sometimes you can be in a different mindset or perhaps your situation has changed and suddenly the things you tried before that didn't work, now do! Leaving your abuser doesn't always mean the abuse stops and recovering from a controlling relationship takes time and effort and practice every day, but you CAN do it and it can be the best thing you ever do.

If you aren't quite there yet, don't panic – start learning and understanding -this knowledge will help you cope better and get stronger until you ARE ready.

Everyone gets the 'lightbulb moment' in their own time - for some it takes a matter of weeks, for some it can take years and unfortunately for some it never happens or it is too late. There is no judgement here – it's your life, you choose which way it goes. Abusive relationships shape you, but they don't have to define you. There is always a way out, but the choice about how, where and when has to be yours and yours alone to make, when the time is right for you.

This book is about creating change. Your controlling partner (ex) is unlikely to change - they are what they are.

Understanding their behaviour is part of processing your experiences, but that knowledge doesn't actually change anything. YOU have to be the change. You have the power! It doesn't matter how long you have been together, it's never too late. I have known women who have been in abusive relationships for over 30 years and who still find happiness afterwards. If you want to make the changes then you absolutely can and I can show you how. Let's take 'Sarah' as an example..

Sarah came to me after being married for over 25 years. Sarah had gone on holiday with her husband only for him to tell her that he wanted a divorce. This completely floored her - she had not seen that coming at all! Sarah hadn't been happy for some time but it was only when we started to unpick things that she realised she had been experiencing emotional abuse for all these years.

It's not been an easy process but over the past few months Sarah has transformed into someone who is confident, embracing her new found independence and is no longer frightened of the future. Sarah is now looking forward to buying a place of her own- she has a new job with financial independence and a new circle of friends.

"We all ate Chinese food on Christmas Day – my ex always liked a traditional dinner, but none of us ever did, but if we objected my ex used to turn it into a big argument.This year we chose what we wanted to eat and we loved it! It might seem like such a small thing but to us it signalled a new beginning."

See what a difference a few months can make?

I wrote this book and set up my own coaching business after years of working with women experiencing domestic abuse, because I wanted to help women who were struggling, as I had done, on their own. Not everyone comes to the attention of police or social care (or wants to!) - so what do they do? How do they get through it? They muddle through as I did, with nobody to offload to, no practical help and no guidance, when they have to make some of the most important decisions in their life.

When I was going through it, domestic abuse was seen as simply that - domestic - nobody else's business. In some ways having nobody else to rely on made me stronger. I created, unwittingly, my own survival toolkit and bit by bit, things got better - but it was slow, and I made mistakes that had repercussions for many years afterwards. This book will help you avoid my mistakes. The quotes and accounts in this book from other women are all real – you are definitely not the only one going through this.

Leaving an abusive relationship is one of the scariest things you can do - it isn't easy, things sometimes seem worse before they get better, but it is worth it. Don't think of yourself as weak – you are strong, you have just been led to believe you are weak, that isn't the same thing. People that survive domestic abuse are some of the strongest people I know.

The world outside of the one you know can be uncertain and challenging but it can also be the place where you find the sunshine again - where you start to laugh again, smile and find a little peace. Imagine how amazing that could be? A place where you don't have to wake up each morning with a sick feeling in your stomach, where you actually enjoy your life, rather than just surviving it. Allow your mind to open up to possibility of that..

I did it, so can you!

I met my first husband when I was 17 years old. A naïve, young girl living away from home, lonely, looking for love in all the wrong places. I didn't recognise the warning signs of abuse at all, had no other relationship to compare it to, and nobody to talk to about it. My ex swept into my life and before I had time to blink, he had moved in and swept me off my feet. I thought it was great, I felt grown up, but what I didn't realise at first was that he was taking over. He controlled everything – who I was allowed to be friends with, what music I listened to, the clothes I wore. Everything was dictated by him and if I dared to challenge, he would sulk for days until I gave in or bully me into submission.

I remember vividly staring out of the window one day, telling myself 'it's ok, it won't always be like this – it will stop, I don't know when, but it will.' I knew I wasn't happy but I didn't know what to do about it. I just didn't know how to explain it to anyone and I didn't know how or when I would be able to get myself out of it. Instead, I learnt how to manage his behaviour and we drifted along.

Before I knew it, 10 years had passed. Getting married didn't make it better, neither did buying a house together or having a baby – in fact it got worse. After a couple of half– hearted attempts to leave I was finally ready. I knew this was it. In a flurry I threw some things in a case, left my home, my belongings, everything behind – it was the scariest thing I had ever done in my life.

I set myself a date to leave and organised it with a friend, so she could hold me accountable. She booked me a train ticket and as soon as he left for work, I got packing. I knew I had to get as far away as I could possibly go so that he couldn't win me round again. My heart was pumping – I was shaking like a leaf. I knew there was no going back. Little did I know that this was the beginning of another chapter that would take years to conclude. I lost everything, including my home and my child. I had no money, was struggling to cope at work and going through a complete and utter nightmare. Of course, it did end, eventually, and in the meantime, I worked out how to manage him and began to build a new life.

There was a turning point when I knew I could no longer feel guilty about something that actually wasn't my fault. I hadn't gone into this relationship hoping that it would end like this. I didn't ask to be abused. Whatever had happened was as a result of his behaviour, not mine. I needed a fresh start, somewhere where there would be no judgement, where people would understand my experiences. I knew there must be other people out there like me, so I trained as one of the first domestic violence specialists in the UK and spent the next 14 years training professionals and working with victims of domestic abuse. Everything I have experienced personally and through my professional training has come together to form my 'Recognition to Recovery' plan. Living with abuse is hard - leaving an abusive relationship is even harder and it can often seem easier to stay than to leave. There will be good days and bad days, things that stress you out, overwhelm you, it's a rollercoaster.

This book will be your guide towards feeling stronger, more in control and to achieving the life you deserve once again. It CAN be done.

This is me just starting out in my nursing career around the same time I met my husband- little did I know what the next few years would hold.

CHAPTER 1:

RECOGNITION

Narcissists, controlling relationships and domestic abuse

What is the difference between these 3 types of abuse?

Is narcissist abuse worse than a controlling relationship?

Is domestic abuse just physical abuse?

The answer is no. Whether you call it narcissist abuse, a controlling relationship or domestic abuse, it's all essentially the same thing. Narcissists are controlling and controlling people often have narcissistic traits. That said, there is a spectrum – from those who display 'mild' emotional abuse, jealousy and controlling behaviour to those who exhibit persistent, obsessive, pre-meditated and sadistic abuse. Abusers are controlled – there is a pattern of behaviour, it is never a 'one-off' incident. It starts off slowly, insidiously, seeping into your relationship without you knowing and then it escalates, getting worse as time goes on and as they get away with it time and time again.

Some professionals who work in this field object to the phrase 'controlling relationship' as they fear it implies both parties are to blame and I understand that, but on the flip side, there are many women who if you asked them if they had experienced domestic abuse, would say no. They still think of domestic abuse as physical – if you don't have a black eye or have to make an excuse about walking into the cupboard door, then it's not abusive, right? Wrong! If you ask someone if they have ever had a jealous or a controlling partner they may say no, but ask them if their ex had ever threatened them they might say "yes, he did that all the time, but he only said it in anger.." Sometimes it is just different wording and phrasing that we use that connects us to our experiences. Most victims don't recognise that what they are experiencing is domestic abuse.

"I wanted to divorce my husband for years, but never had the courage and I don't know why. He never even asked me to marry him, I didn't have a choice – he just told my parents and that was that. All these years he has just done what he wanted to do and I just put up with it. I won't put up with it anymore."

I read many posts on social media where women are asking questions about exactly the type of personality disorder their ex has and comparing notes with other women in similar situations. It's not a competition about whose ex was the worst?! While this can give you some reassurance that you aren't alone, it doesn't help to focus on the 'why's' and trying to diagnose them. Does it really matter if your partner is a 'toxic narcissist' or a 'closet narcissist'? It doesn't change your situation if you know that. The behaviour is still happening, you just have a label for it. It's useful to be able to recognise the tactics, to understand the intention behind them, but your focus remains on the abuser whilst you do that.

Instead, focus your intention on you:

'How does this person make me feel?

What needs to change?

What do I deserve?

What causes abusive behaviour?

Well first of all, what doesn't? It's not caused by a bad childhood, a bad day at work, a bad temper, a 'red mist' or anything at all other than 'choice'. If it was caused by any of these influences, then the abuser would be abusive to other people too, not just you, and all alcoholics would be abusers and all people with mental health would be abusive to their partners. They would have no idea why they abuse and wouldn't be able to control it. Drugs, alcohol and unstable mental health can all be triggers to incidents, but they are not the root cause.

The brutal truth is that abusers DO know what they are doing, they know the reaction they are going to get and they CHOOSE to abuse in order to get their own way. Most abusers are in fact cowards, who intentionally bully and abuse behind closed doors where they feel the most powerful and where they can 'get away with it', not in public where they will be more visible. Note how they can be completely charming when they want to be! They can turn it on and off as and when it suits them.

"My ex is so charming to everyone else. He has a good job, wears a suit, knows how to speak and completely controls every meeting I have to attend. I am shaking in my boots and he is there with a big grin on his face, pointing the finger at me, trying to convince everyone else it is my fault or that I am exaggerating. Why can't they see it's all an act?"

Abusers thrive on feeling untouchable. Their sense of self-importance knows no bounds, they have no fear of repercussions and consequences. Alarm bells should ring even louder when abusers abuse their partner outside of the home and show no regard for consequences. When an abuser is abusing in public, they simply don't care who sees them. Their intention is to frighten, shame and bully their victim into agreeing with them and they do this in public to increase the power of their intimidation. If you see someone physically or emotionally abusing someone in public, imagine what they are doing at home, where nobody can see or hear them ...

"My ex got caught with his hands around my throat after we were out in town. Luckily someone called the police but I had to lie and say I was ok. I became a very good liar when I was with him. I knew if I didn't make the lie convincing, then I would be in more trouble."

Having a bad childhood can leave you with 'attachment issues' and fear of abandonment. Abusers may copy abusive behaviour because they think that is the normal way to behave, having grown up witnessing it with their parents, but ultimately abusing someone else is a choice. They know what they are doing. They know what they want to achieve and they go 'all out' to get it, with no regard for how it makes you feel. They may 'forget' to take their medication for their mental health, because they know this makes them more unpredictable or volatile. Assaults may happen after the abuser has had a few drinks, but alcohol is not the cause. Alcohol may trigger an assault or an escalation in abuse, because the drinker is less inhibited, but the intention to abuse is already there — the alcohol just lets it all spill out. You may want to believe that there is some underlying cause, some reason that will explain why your partner is treating you so badly, that if they can only get help for these triggers, the abuse will stop, but unfortunately the only reason they are being abusive is because they are choosing to.

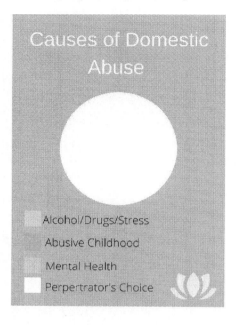

Causes of Domestic Abuse

- Alcohol/Drugs/Stress
- Abusive Childhood
- Mental Health
- Perpertrator's Choice

Many women feel they are partly to blame for the abuse, 'just as bad as him'. They may lash out at him, even hit back, try and provoke him. This behaviour makes everything more confusing and often stops them from seeking help. You are NOT as bad as him. You are NOT an abuser. You ARE a victim crying out to be heard. You are simply wanting the abuse to stop. When someone puts you down persistently every day, for years and years, your emotions are stifled. You 'put a lid on it' because you are afraid to challenge, to question, to speak up because you know to do so will make things worse. Like a fizzy bottle of pop, being shaken time and time again, it will explode eventually. The anger, the resentment you feel at being treated so badly, has to come out somehow. This does NOT mean that you are abusive too, you are simply trying to regain some control and be heard. The intention behind your behaviour is completely different. Your abuser is the only person to blame for the abuse. The end.

"My children asked me why I was shouting and I realised that I wasn't shouting, but my voice was loud. I was simply trying to be heard."

" He was going downstairs and I just kicked him in the back, making him lose his footing on the stairs. There was no deep thought behind it, I just felt so angry in that moment and wanted to lash out at him, to give him a taste of his own medicine, to show him how angry I was at what he was doing to me. Of course, he flipped! I have never seen his face so full of rage and he pinned me by my throat to the wall. I never did that again."

Every abusive relationship is slightly different but there are many similar tactics that abusers use and beliefs that are so similar. You make think these statements are unique to you, but they aren't. If you can recognise the things they say as tactics, understand how they fit in with the abuser's belief system, then you can learn how to protect yourself from them in future. Everything they say will be designed to manipulate you into agreeing with what they want – when they are nice, it is not genuine, just another tactic to lull you into a false sense of security.

Abusers essentially believe that they are better than you – more important, more clever, more powerful, there is no equal partnership here! They believe that they can't cope without you, that when they behave badly, it is because you made them do it, it is because they can't help it, they believe that you will leave and they will be alone. They believe they are the best you will ever get, that they deserve thanks for putting up with you, that they saved you. Of course, none of this is true, it is what they tell themselves to justify their actions. They try to make you believe it too, because then you won't leave and things can carry on just the way they are.

Rules to live by

The abuser will have their own set of rules that you have to live by. Some may be unspoken rules, and each rule will change on a regular basis. These rules prevent you from having any sense of calm and order in your life. You never know when these rules might change, you have no say in these rules. They need to let you know who is in charge – if you break the rules there can be consequences and that in turn will help them justify their behaviour.

When the rules are broken or they think something is about to change (such as you leaving) they have to adapt quickly to remind you know who is boss. They believe you need to be controlled. This is 'danger time', when controlling behaviour can escalate into physical or sexual abuse and they let you know in no uncertain terms that you need to obey the rules. The abuser is desperate and in times of desperation, fear of consequences goes out of the window. They must keep control at all costs.

You will have rules about who you are allowed to talk to, who controls the money, who does the childcare, how you must speak. Within those sets of rules will be smaller sub-rules and those rules will change frequently and without notice or discussion.

"I always had to cook for him – he would never cook for me, even though he could. I was always told not to tell my mum anything about our home life. He always had to bath the kids and I wasn't allowed in there, which used to upset me as I thought bath-time would be a time for us all to play together as a family. Looking back, there were so many rules, but I just went along with them for a quiet life."

Minimising, denying and blaming

- I only did it because I love you sooo much.

- It wasn't that bad – you are exaggerating!

- You are frigid – no wonder you never had a boyfriend before me.

- I have to do everything because you are too stupid to do it

- I will get help. I will commit to counselling.

- If you leave, I won't be able to cope. I will kill myself. I have nothing left to live for, I will kill you, I will take the kids, I will screw you over financially.

- I never did that – you're making it up. I told you, you are mental!

"My ex used to tell me I was so clever – I had a great job, a very important job, he knew I loved it. I used to feel good when he gave me compliments but then he would also tell me I couldn't cook because I was too useless at it and that I couldn't manage our finances because he was far smarter than me. This made me doubt myself and he would always say why are you doing this to me? Like it was my fault!"

They will shift the blame, blaming anyone and everyone except themselves. They believe that their behaviour was ok –they don't understand why we question it. They will try to convince you that it wasn't nearly as bad as you are suggesting or may even blatantly lie and deny that anything actually happened. They have to find somebody to blame – if they can't find anyone to blame then they have to look at their own behaviour and accept responsibility for it, and that is never going to happen! The vast majority of abusers don't see they have a problem with their behaviour, which makes it nigh on impossible to change. Abusers have a very long list of excuses, justifications and people they can blame for their behaviour.

They definitely don't believe in equal rights! Their way is always better, they are far more superior, intelligent, and always right, never wrong. Remember the nursery rhyme

'King of the Castle'? You are the dirty rascal. All couples and families have unwritten rules about domestic chores, based on their abilities, their age, their preferences, their working hours, etc – without these rules there would indeed be chaos and these rules ensure a fair distribution of workload. After all, it takes a huge amount of effort to keep a home running smoothly!

In my house one of our unwritten rules is that I do the cooking and my husband washes up – he hates cooking, I don't mind it. I do most of the housework but he takes care of the finances - I hate this and he is much better at it than I am. I have access to my own account, to spend how I wish, without having to justify it. You work out a way between you that helps your home and your family life run smoothly. There are jobs everyone hates doing, but we do them without making a big deal of it.

We also all have things that niggle us about our partners – the way they leave their socks on the floor or the way they reload the dishwasher when you have already done it – these things irritate us, but it's not a major problem. We don't worry about challenging their behaviour and sometimes choose to simply ignore it, because in the grand scheme of things, it's a minor irritation – we know above all they love us, care for us and this is a genuine, equal partnership. Nobody is perfect!

The 'King of the Castle' however, has very clear rules – the dinner has to be ready by a certain time, you have to dress a certain way, the children have to be quiet when he gets home from work -as his job is VERY important and even though you may have been at home with the children all day and be in dire need of some help, he needs to relax, so you had better look after him! The abuser believes that he is far more valuable and important and clever than we are and will do his upmost to let us know that at every given opportunity. He criticises and belittles us, chipping away at our confidence and we stay.

"Everything had to be his way –he dictated everything. None of us had a choice, he booked holidays without involving me or the kids. He took us on the types of holidays he wanted and pushed the kids to do things he wanted them to do, but the kids hated it. He always ended up shouting at me for being too stupid to read a map, we would inevitably arrive late and stressed and the kids would be fed up before the holiday had even started!"

If an abuser feels they are losing control they will enlist help. They will use the children - the most powerful of tools. They will tug at your heart, convince you that the children need both parents when you try to leave. They will blame you for calling the police and tell the children they will go to jail because of you, they will buy the children expensive gifts they know you can't afford to buy, to gain favour with the children. Children become pawns in their game and we will explore this in more detail in a while.

So, if that is what an abuser does, what might a healthy, loving relationship look like? Caring, supportive, fun, equal, responsible, able to admit when they are wrong, encouraging. All of this and more! Do you think these are words that would describe your partner or ex??

Power and Control and Tactics

Domestic abuse is a pattern of behaviour; the Government definition is:

Any incident or pattern of incidents of controlling, coercive or threatening behaviour, violence or abuse between those aged 16 or over who are or have been intimate partners or family members regardless of gender or sexuality. This can encompass but is not limited to the following types of abuse:

- Psychological/Emotional
- Physical

- Sexual

- Financial/Economic

- Using the Children

- Isolation

It's quite a lot to encompass in a definition, isn't it?! That's because it is sooo complex. In some relationships there are times when the abuser becomes the victim and the victim becomes the abuser, but at the core of it there is still one person who is trying to keep the other down and one trying to rise up.

In these relationships there is usually some element of co-dependence and they are often very chaotic, sometimes with drugs/alcohol/mental health involved. Domestic abuse can involve abuse from someone other than your spouse – it might be a sibling, your son, or other family members. For the purposes of this book, I will focus on intimate relationships with a spouse, a partner or an ex. Whether you are married makes no difference, only in terms of legal Rights and options, but other than that, everything is the same. Abuse can also happen to anyone – I have supported police officers, teachers, social workers, solicitors. When you are emotionally invested you have your blinkers on. All your professional knowledge goes out the window! You may feel worried that your colleagues will find out or feel embarrassed that you should have been able to see the signs. Don't be – you are only human and you are entitled to the same help as everyone else.

Controlling behaviour is: *'a range of acts designed to make a person subordinate and/or dependent by isolating them from sources of support, exploiting their resources and capacities for personal gain, depriving them of the means needed for independence, resistance and escape and regulating their everyday behaviour.'* In a nutshell, this means that by controlling your movements, who you speak to, connect with, by taking away your ability to have any choice over anything, the abuser's tactics become all the more powerful. This is NOT an equal, respectful relationship!

Coercive behaviour is: *'an act or a pattern of acts of assault, threats, humiliation and intimidation or other abuse that is used to harm, punish, or frighten their victim.'* Your abuser threatens, bullies or persuades you to do things that you may not necessarily agree to do if you weren't frightened of repercussions. The fear of what might happen if you say 'no' convinces you to do whatever your abuser says.

This definition of domestic abuse, includes so called 'honour' based abuse, where a victim is worried about bringing shame on their family, female genital mutilation and forced marriage, where victims are coerced or forced into marriage. In these situations where there may be additional challenges as you try to access support. What happens if you can't read, you don't understand the legal system in the UK you risk being shunned by your family and your whole community if you leave or report your abuser? Like I said before there is no excuse for abuse and although there may be extra challenges that come with leaving your abuser in these situations, you can do it. There are organisations that can help with these types of abuse – see the list at the back of this book.

This next list details some tactics that abusers use, but is absolutely not exclusive -these are some of the most common ones. I can't tell you how many times I have heard of these ones over the years, you are definitely not alone if you recognise any of these. It's honestly like they all went to some secret school for abusers!

Psychological Abuse

Emotional abuse that affects your mental state and memory. It can include a variety of tactics that brainwash you into submission, including:

Isolation

Preventing you from having contact with friends/family / colleagues. The quicker they can isolate you, the more control they have and everyone else who comes into contact with you is a threat. Isolation is usually one of the first tactics abusers use – it is so powerful! Anyone who potentially could open your eyes to the reality of your situation, who may offer you a way out, spells danger to an abuser, so they will do anything and everything to keep you to themselves. They may offer to move the family home to somewhere that sounds amazing – when things get worse you suddenly realise that you are hundreds of miles away from your friends and family and totally disconnected from anyone who could help you. They may subtly make it known that they object every time your friends come over, stomping around being moody and ignorant in front of your them or ignoring them and creating an uncomfortable atmosphere.

What do you do then? You make excuses for him, you stop inviting them and without even knowing it, you isolate yourself. Your abuser may work out how long it takes you to travel there and back to your mum's and 'allow' you an hour to see her, sending you txt messages just to remind you to hurry up. You may feel embarrassed at the constant interruptions, so become secretive about your family meetings or just stop going. Your abuser may offer to go with you every time you go to the GP for your depression - seemingly supportive but really there to prevent any opportunity for you to speak up.

" I had been invited to my sister's local pub for the evening. By the time I got home he was drunk. He had clearly been winding himself up all evening so he was raging by the time I returned. He started an argument, he told me I clearly didn't love him and spent the next 3 hours ranting about how my family hated me and he didn't understand why I wanted to see them anyway. I just stopped going out and made excuses – it was easier than having to deal with the aftermath."

Distorted Beliefs

More lies, justifications and excuses to convince themselves (and you) that this behaviour is ok, that it is normal. They actually start to believe their own lies, as it helps them feel better about what they have done. They shift the blame on to you, they persuade you that they are 'only doing it to protect you', because they love you so much, because they can't help it. *"I only did it because...* (insert any old excuse here).

The abuser will accuse you of exaggerating, of being over-dramatic or causing the incident. Of course, what this particular tactic also does, is get you to question your own behaviour. You start doubting yourself – did I cause it? Am I exaggerating? Maybe I should be glad they love me so deeply!

"It wasn't that bad! You are sooo sensitive! I only mentioned that we were late because you needed so much time to get ready – after all it takes a lot of work since you had the kids! You know you have put on weight. I don't understand why you had to go and make a scene! Now I can't even face them, you are going to have to go and apologise for your behaviour. You are such an embarrassment!"

" I will leave if you want me to, but I hope you don't have another breakdown. You won't be able to cope with the kids on your own, you couldn't cope last time you left - you know I have to help you with everything. Even your mum says you are hopeless and she can't understand how I put up with you!"

Am I to blame? Was it my fault?

Was it as bad as I thought? Am I exaggerating?

NO. Remember, the blame for abuse lies solely with the abuser. It doesn't matter what you did or didn't do, what you said or didn't say, it's never justification for abuse. They can choose to agree to disagree with you, to be respectful towards you, to walk away, but they don't.

Threats

When they can't persuade you that their way is the right way, or even worse, they suspect you are on the verge of leaving, the threats come in. Threats frighten you, even if you are not sure if they are true. The fear stops you from speaking out, from telling people what is really going on - you are not sure if anyone will believe you, you are not sure if you even believe it yourself. Your abuser knows your worst fears and use them to keep you there.

They threaten to take your children, to 'screw you over financially', to hound you if you leave, to tell lies about you to other people, to send intimate photos of you to your family. You have no idea if they will ever follow through with the threats, but do you want to take that chance? Their body language can be enough to send you into a spin - that 'look in his eye' that means trouble.

" If you leave me it will be the last thing you do and don't even think about coming after me for money because I would rather see you in the gutter than give you a penny. If you leave, I will kill myself – explain THAT to the kids!"

Exhaustion

The abuser deprives you of sleep, waking you up on purpose in the middle of the night, to have sex or make them food, before moaning about the fact that you are always tired. They force you to do impossible tasks, they constantly demand attention, they make you redo housework until it meets their standards, leaving you no time to yourself. The mental exhaustion of 'walking on eggshells' and constantly trying to manage your abuser's behaviour is debilitating. It is all you think about.

Trying not to react to the constant criticism is exhausting. Trying to protect the children from hearing and seeing his behaviour means you are constantly trying to be two steps ahead of him. If you can't think straight because you are so damn tired, how can you possibly summon up enough energy to even start thinking about how to leave?

"My ex used to hide bits of paper underneath the pictures and check if they had moved. If they hadn't, it meant I hadn't cleaned properly and he would make me do it again while he supervised. I had to cook for him any time he wanted - even if he had to wake me up to do it."

Occasional Indulgences

These are the little treats to keep you sweet. The bunch of flowers, the 'help' around the house, the pledges of undying love and promises to change, promises it will never happen again, the holidays booked (with your credit card!) so you can have some quality time together. They panic when things start to go wrong, when they worry you might leave, so they have to get in quick and tug at your heartstrings. They do something nice or say something nice to reel you back in again.

You remember the times when you first got together. You hold on to the hope that things will get better and you start to believe it. Of course, these romantic gestures are NOT genuine, they will do whatever it takes to get things back to normal, quickly! They won't want things to change – they just want you to believe that they will, so you stay.

" He always seemed to know when I was getting close to leaving – he would book time away for us with the kids and make sure we had a great time. He knew this was all I had ever wanted for my family, but then once we were home, the criticism and the comments would start all over again. He would also buy the kids everything they wanted, treat them to things he knew I wouldn't be able to afford if I left. How could I deprive the kids of those things?"

Superior Power

Displays of total power to create absolute fear and terror. The bully who bulks himself out at the gym, who spits in your face, who pins you to the wall by your throat in a rage. The bully who leaves knives and weapons out for you to see, just so you know they are there any time they should choose to use them.

From time to time, you may become brave and stand up to them, but you are sure to regret it. The repercussions of your objection may be worse than the incident which caused you to object in the first place. The bully ensures you never attempt to do that again. They shake their foot, tap their fingers, stomp around the house, punch walls, slam doors, talk through gritted teeth, clench their fists.

"He used to get that look in his eye and I knew there was going to be trouble. I was a petite size 10 and he was 6'2" muscly and overpowering - how could I stand up to him when he was angry? He was literally twice the size of me"

Humiliation and degradation

The way they embarrass you in front of friends, make inappropriate comments about you or your relationship in front of other people, brag about how amazing they are and how stupid you are, cause a scene at family events. These actions are all about causing you embarrassment. Abusing you in public just compounds the shame that you feel. What do you do so it doesn't happen again? You stop socialising, you turn down invitations, you make excuses. I once had a client whose hair was her crowning glory, so what did her abuser do? Force her to chop it short. He knew this would affect her confidence, and in his mind, this made her seem less attractive to other men and therefore less likely to leave him.

I have known of other men insisting that their partners dye their hair a particular colour to make them easily recognisable in a crowd – so they have no hiding place. Humiliation plays havoc with your sense of self, your body image, your sense of self-worth and many victims who experience these particular forms of abuse feel too ashamed to even speak about them.

Again, this is about power and control – the need to make you feel that you can't leave, as who would want you now anyway? The abuser wants you to feel ashamed, dirty, worthless, but you are not. You have nothing to feel ashamed of. The shame is the abuser's shame. You don't have to physically hurt someone to have them under your control. Psychological abuse is brainwashing and it is powerful stuff.

"My ex threw a pint of beer over me in the middle of the pub. Of all the things he did to me, even comparing it to the times he punched me, this was the worst. I have never felt so humiliated in my life and the fact it was in front of my family was even worse."

Physical Abuse

Punching, hair pulling (often during sex just to show you who is the boss), choking/strangulation. There is a spectrum of seriousness with this type of behaviour – from poking you every time you walk past to wind you up, right up to the ultimate abuse, murder. Strangulation and stabbing remain the two most common ways that women die as a result of domestic abuse and there have been several cases where men have used the excuse 'it was just a sex game gone wrong' to excuse their behaviour.

People experiencing physical abuse also make excuses, they cover up, they hide the bruises and they hide away from anyone who may suspect what is really going on. Physical abuse often comes into play when the coercive and controlling behaviour isn't having as much effect as the abuser wants it to – they have to up their game.

"I left a divorce leaflet on the table just so he knew I was leaving this time and that I wasn't prepared to put up with

any more of his shit. I felt strong and I wanted to show him. Stupid really, he got so angry he pushed me on the floor, ripped my wedding ring off and stamped on my head. I fled to a neighbour and called police. I never thought he would do something like that."

Emotional Abuse

''Put-downs', criticisms, name-calling, lying, dismissing their behaviour as 'not that bad', blaming you for causing arguments or making mistakes. Emotional abuse encompasses anything your partner says to intentionally make you feel bad about yourself, to destroy your confidence and self-esteem, to make you doubt your abilities.

This can include 'gaslighting' where an abuser will lie to cover up their behaviour and make you question your own sanity: *'no I never said that to you/ did that, you must have dreamt that up, you must be losing your mind'*. You question your own sense of reality and you can even start to become convinced that you are indeed mentally ill and that it is you that has the problem.

'' My ex used to hide things and then when I couldn't find them, he would convince me that I had thrown them out or lost them. He would completely deny that arguments had even happened. I thought I was going mad! He thought it was funny."

Emotional abuse is always present when there is abuse in a relationship as it is the most powerful of all the tactics. Many people say that the emotional abuse can actually be worse than the physical. It's difficult to forget the hurtful words said to you, you can't unhear them. Bruises fade, but you never completely forget the words said to you.

Abusers can be cruel – they will taunt you, call you names and constantly put you down. Even after you separate, they will try and find a way to emotionally abuse you – the trick is to not let them. You can't control what they say, but you CAN filter them and make sure that the words don't hurt you like they used to.

"He used to call me stupid all the time. He would criticise every little thing I did. Nothing was ever good enough. I still found it really difficult after we separated - he used to email me about the children but there would always be some criticism in there. A sentence or two just so he could have a little dig again. I now get my friend to read his emails, so I don't have to. I realised I don't have to listen to him anymore."

Sexual abuse

Again, there is a spectrum of abuse, from forcing you or persuading you to do sexual acts you wouldn't normally agree to do right up to rape. Many women find the concept of rape confusing when it happens within the context of a marital relationship. It was only in 1991 that marital rape became illegal in the UK and many people still think that because you are married, that automatically gives your husband the right to have sex however and whenever he wants – 'conjugal rights'.

They are wrong. 'No' means 'No', that's it. Simple. You have a right to say no, any time you want to. If you are also under the influence of alcohol or drugs or don't have mental capacity, then you automatically lose the ability to consent freely as far as UK criminal law is concerned.

"My ex used to question me incessantly, convinced I was having an affair. I wasn't allowed to look up when we went out because that meant I was flirting. He encouraged me to fantasise about other men even though I didn't want to, so I just used to lie, because that was the only way to stop him going on. All it did was make him more convinced I was attracted to other men. If he caught me so much as smiling at another man he would force me to have sex to 'prove my love for him' me when we got home."

Sexual abuse is a powerful form of abuse – being forced or persuaded to watch pornography, dress up in overtly sexy clothes, being forced to have sex when you have only recently given birth or had surgery are just some examples. Another way in which an abuser can use sex as a weapon to hurt us, is by with-holding sex or affection. When you are craving a bit of love, desperate to hear something, feel something, that proves your partner loves and cares for you, they blank you, turn their back on you, blame you for them not wanting to have sex with you, they threaten to go and have sex with escort girls instead of you, they ignore your pleas for affection. Sexual abuse is a powerful tool in the abuser's armoury.

"My ex used to call me frigid when I didn't want to have sex with him. He used to bully me into wearing sexy underwear which made me feel cheap and tarty. He used to tell me he would go and have sex with other women if I didn't do what he asked. I used to think to myself – go on, please do! That would have given me the excuse I needed to leave him, but of course he didn't. I spent years just doing what I had to do to get the sex over and done with as quickly as possible."

Financial/Economic abuse

This will now be included within the new Domestic Abuse Bill coming into UK law in 2021 as it is now widely recognised as one of the most common tactics of domestic abuse used against victims, particularly women. Agreeing for your spouse to control all the finances may have seemed a good idea at the time, but if you want to leave, it makes you incredibly vulnerable. You may not have your own bank account, you may have no independent income, no access to ready cash.

This imbalance when it comes to finances leaves the abuser in an extremely powerful position – you may have to ask your abuser for money, even for basic items, you may have to account for every penny spent, showing receipts and mileage for essential journeys and you may have to justify every purchase you make.

What happens if the children are in private school and then your ex decides they don't want to pay for it any more just to spite you? Do you know how to budget if you leave? Do you know whether you will be able to afford to live in the marital home if you end your relationship?

Lack of control and independence related to finances can leave you with limited options and feeling completely trapped should you want to leave your abuser. Finances and housing worries are the two main reasons why people stay in abusive relationships – they have no idea how to survive if they leave.

"My husband and I discussed having a trial separation, so he moved out. Within 2 weeks he had bought himself a flat using savings from our joint account without my knowledge. He bought himself a new car, filed for divorce and told me 'don't even think about coming after me for my money'. I was left with no income, no way of knowing how I was going to pay the bills and 2 young children to support. To say I was shocked was an under-statement. After 23 years of marriage, I never thought he would be so brutal."

Stalking and harassment

Many victims think that there has to be a long history of harassment before you can report it to police -that is not the case. In fact, you only have to have 2 incidents of unwanted or persistent contact from your ex before this is classified in criminal law as harassment.

Stalking is a specific type of persistent harassment where the abuser is obsessive and often feels very aggrieved or 'hard done by' - they will make several attempts to convince you and others that you should still be together in a relationship or they will seek revenge because they feel so distraught that you have left. They may turn up at events unexpectedly, they may contact your friends, family, employer, ex-partner, neighbour, trying to find out more information about you or trying to persuading others to help you reconcile. Stalkers obsess about their victim day and night. You are all they think about – you are the most important thing in their world, even if you have only been together for a short time.

They will send gifts declaring undying love or they will threaten to hurt you if you don't give in to their demands. Above all, they want to be with you – they won't take no for an answer and they will do whatever it takes to try and convince you that you will be better off with them than without them. If you are being stalked you need professional help – these are dangerous abusers and you need a safety plan and support, don't try to manage this alone.

Narcissistic Traits

Here are a few you might recognise!

- A grandiose sense of self-importance. They are sooo much better, cleverer/smarter/stronger than everyone else!

- Deluded fantasies about earning loads of money, being able to buy an amazing house, get an amazing promotion at work, etc. even though the reality is that they can't hold down a job and have no money!

- They always need admiration and reassurance from you about how much you love them – it's never enough, they need a constant supply.

- Lack of empathy – absolutely! They never understand how their behaviour affects other people. It's always someone else's fault, there is always some excuse or something they can use to justify their behaviour.

- They feel 'hard done by' – they feel they deserve better and are envious of others. They are forever feeling sorry for themselves.

- They are arrogant and love to exploit others – they feel they can 'get away with it' and it makes them feel good when they do it.

If you recognise these traits in your partner, then you are wasting your time trying to fix them. In order for someone to change, they have to first of all recognise they have a problem. Narcissists and people with controlling traits choose not to see that they have a problem, so they are falling at the first hurdle. Don't waste your time trying to fix them. They chose you because you are full of empathy – because you can feed them with their constant need for attention, but exactly what are you getting out of this relationship?

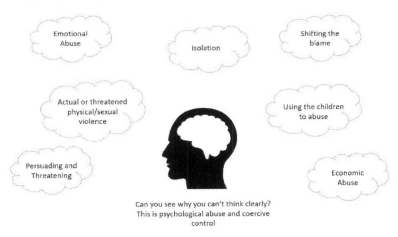

Emotional Abuse

Isolation

Shifting the blame

Actual or threatened physical/sexual violence

Using the children to abuse

Persuading and Threatening

Economic Abuse

Can you see why you can't think clearly? This is psychological abuse and coercive control

Do you recognise any of these behaviours in your relationship?

How an abusive relationship develops

The main question to ask yourself right now is how does my partner make me feel?

No excuses, be completely 100% honest with yourself. You don't necessarily need to make any decisions at all at this point, just explore and figure out where you are with your relationship and see if you can recognise any of the abusive behaviours I have just listed.

Can you count up how many you can connect with? Can you think of examples?

Flip to the back of this book to see the relationship balance tool.

Which side of the page is your relationship on?

Some of the tactics that abusers use, are very obvious, but some are also very subtle - after all, if they used the most obvious ones straight away, the relationship wouldn't last very long, would it? If your new partner punched you in the face on a second date would you go back for more? I doubt it!

Lovebombing

They are very clever – the abusive behaviour slowly seeps in drip by drip. In the beginning they use a powerful technique called 'lovebombing' to persuade you into believing that this relationship is everything you ever wanted. They tell you everything you want to hear, you think they are amazing, charming, special, they make you feel fantastic, loved, secure, until you have totally immersed yourself in this relationship. You have fallen head over heels in love and your commitment to them is absolute.

Slowly but surely the abusive tactics begin to creep in - very subtly, so you don't even notice them. A niggling doubt you have when they criticise you for the first time, out of the blue, completely uncalled for, and the first time you have to make an excuse for their behaviour. These are warning signs that something is wrong, but we choose to ignore it. Not only do we ignore it but we change our behaviour so that it doesn't happen again. After all this relationship is the best thing that has ever happened to us, so we will do whatever it takes to make it work. Of course, at this point we are also assuming we are to blame and that any cracks in the relationship are also our fault.

We question ourselves – did I do something wrong?

What can I do to put it right? What can I do to get back to how things were in the beginning?

"In the beginning it was amazing! I really thought I had landed on my feet. He had an amazing job, a lovely family, he doted on me – took me to amazing places, told me everything I wanted to hear. The first time I thought something was wrong was when he told me off for laughing too loudly at one of his friends jokes. He accused me of flirting, which I wasn't, I was just having a good time, but then every time that friend was there, he made sure I knew he was monitoring me. I made sure I ignored his friend and didn't laugh at anything he said. It was so subtle, but I should have questioned it then and trusted my instincts instead of being completely charmed and taken in by him."

Now we are also **'walking on eggshells'** – trying to predict our partner's mood trying to keep everything calm and putting our partner's needs way above our own – by this point we have forgotten what our needs are! We lose our voice as we would most likely get shouted down anyway, so we stop bothering. We make sure the house is tidy, the kids are quiet, we have sex when we don't want to and we spend all our waking moments trying to keep our partner happy. We creep around the house so we don't disturb them, we redo things over and over again in case we get in trouble for not doing them properly, we exhaust ourselves trying to keep our partner happy.

Of course, this is completely unachievable. The **'rules of the game'** change – sometimes on a daily basis, even on an hourly basis! What kept them happy one day, suddenly changes, so we can't win. If they liked cottage pie on a Monday, the next time we serve it up we are told it's 'slop' and it gets thrown straight in the bin or against the wall and we are subjected to a barrage of abuse about how rubbish a cook we are and how we are trying to poison them. If our partner encourages us to fantasise during sex, they will then throw it back and accuse us of having affairs or call us names to make us feel dirty. If our partner encourages us to tell them our innermost secrets, our fears, our worries, they will use them against us later on – they have the ammunition to shoot us down.

The cycle continues – the build -up of tension, your partner gets wound up over whatever it is you have done wrong this time. You can see your partner tapping their foot, huffing and puffing, stomping around to make a point, getting 'that look in his eye' and you just know something bad is going to happen. Something triggers an incident – it could be something, it could be nothing. To be honest, they don't need an excuse. You waste your breath trying to reason with them, trying to make them see your point of view, trying to placate them, but nothing works. They become angry and it all comes to an explosive crescendo.

Afterwards there are apologies, promises, tears, calm, more apologies, kindness (oh how we have waited for that) and things are better for a while, before the whole cycle starts again. We hang on to the hope that things will continue this way – maybe this is it, maybe they really mean it this time. The things they say are lies designed to give you hope, to stop you from leaving, to shift the blame and to ensure that things carry on as 'normal'.

All of this is exhausting, as we try desperately to keep on top of the ever- increasing list of demands and rules. Our anxiety levels increase to the point where we are so anxious that we can't sleep, we can't switch off, no matter how hard we try. We sleep because we are exhausted and then we are accused of being lazy. If we aren't careful, we can veer towards the wrong kind of coping strategies to take the edge of the daily stress.

Before we know it the odd glass of wine becomes a bottle, we stop eating because we can't digest food properly due to stress or because we don't want to be called 'fat' yet again so we develop an eating disorder. Of course, we think these things help us cope, but over time they actually make us feel worse and of course they give our partner more ammunition as they then threaten to report us for being mentally ill or tell us we can't cope because we have a 'drink problem'.

So, this 'walking on eggshells' continues - we conform. We 'put up and shut up' no matter what. We make excuses for our partner, we ignore the bad behaviour and cling onto those little 'nuggets of niceness', those little glimmers of hope that remind us of how things used to be. We feel grateful to receive a bunch of flowers, (usually after an argument), an offer to 'help' with childcare (for their own children!), the treat of a date night - with a few comments about our weight to keep us on our toes and an expectation of sex at the end of the night.

These are the little treats we cling on to, like an expectant puppy waiting to be thrown a bone for being a good boy. Nothing comes for free. There is always something they want in return or there is always an underlying motive – to prevent you from leaving, to influence other people or to make you doubt your own judgement. Why would you be unhappy when your partner goes out of his way to spoil you, you should be grateful?!

Can you recognise these forms of emotional abuse?

The Mood Killer – he always wants to kill your mood. He is never happy and hates it when you are. They spoil your mood whenever possible because they thrive when you are sad.

Name Calling – a powerful way to put you down and even more powerful when done in front of other people

Mr. Always Right – they never apologise or enter into a discussion about their behaviour, because they are never wrong!

Blame – it's always someone else's fault, never theirs

Jokes – always at your expense. Another way to criticise you or make you feel stupid

Attacking your interests – because these are a threat. They will never support you with anything that brings you joy

Disrespect – to make you feel worthless

You may have heard of the expression **'trauma bonding'**. This describes the confusion between love and emotional abuse. It happens because of the impact of psychological abuse– trauma bonding is why many survivors struggle to recognise abuse in the first place and why it takes victims so long to leave their abuser. The 'lovebombing' completely overwhelms you, this relationship is like no other – toxic, passionate, all-consuming. Abuse feels like love, the love you are desperate for. You believe you aren't enough, that this love has saved you and you are nothing without it.

Your 'knight in shining armour' promises you the world – it's intoxicating, it's passionate, it's everything. To give that up would leave you with nothing, so you stay, even though it hurts. You stay because of the fantasy that things will get better, the belief that they only do it because they love you so much – they know this and they tell you the things you want to hear, you believe them. You minimise and excuse their behaviour because you are desperately trying to please them and get their approval that you are good enough.

When we can't leave, we criticise ourselves – we think we are stupid, that we must deserve it, that if we do leave, we will be alone forever. They reinforce this belief by telling us repeatedly that nobody will love us again, that even our own family don't love us and that we will never cope on our own.

'' *I work as a professional, I work with victims of domestic abuse, yet I couldn't see what he was doing to me. Even though he was abusing me on a daily basis, I was so in love with him. I had risked everything to be with him and was completely head over heels in love. I couldn't turn to anyone, I felt so ashamed and embarrassed and couldn't understand why I still wanted to be with someone who treated me so badly.''*

All of this is exhausting, confusing and debilitating. It stops us from thinking clearly, it makes us feel as if it is our fault, as if we are selfish and ultimately it stops us from leaving. We accept this is how it is. We stop challenging. We stay quiet. We withdraw from everyone, we don't want them to see how bad it is, to see how rubbish we feel, we put on a brave face. We focus on helping others, on working, on the children, on anything to distract us from the reality of our situation or we feel suicidal, because life without them isn't worth living. We feel jealous of others who are happy, but we have no fight left in us. We give in. If we free ourselves from our abuser, we feel guilty, we feel lost, we miss our abuser and we feel ashamed...

..until our '**lightbulb moment**'. Ta da! We start to open our eyes and ears to what is happening. There comes a point when that acceptance and sense of inevitability gradually changes and we begin to feel a growing sense of resentment, frustration, anger and unfairness. We start to feel angry at being treated like this, angry at ourselves for putting up with it, angry at the effect it is having on us and the children. We look at our partner and start to despise them for treating us like this – they are supposed to love you and care for us, not hurt us!

If you plunge a frog into a pan of boiling water it will immediately jump out. If you put it in a pan of tepid water and turn the heat up gradually it will sit quite happily until it has boiled, to death, without even noticing the danger.

Like the 'drip-drip' effect when the abuse starts, now the 'drip-drip' effect of reality sets in. The words that used to frighten us or make us feel bad about ourselves hurt less - we hear them for what they are, words designed to punish us for something that isn't our fault, words designed to make us feel bad when actually we don't have anything to feel bad about. We see our partner for the cruel bully that they are. We feel less intimidated, we dare to answer back or refuse to give in to their demands. We may even laugh out loud at their deluded beliefs. This is a tipping point in the dynamics of our relationship, so we need to be careful here. If we challenge too much we risk being hurt even more, so this is the time to start thinking smart.

There may be something that triggers this primal urge in us, our situation might change or we just start to feel stronger and cope better. Pregnancy is often a trigger for abuse to get worse, but also often the trigger for victims to leave. When you are pregnant there are more people than ever involved in your life – health professionals, more visits from family members, new support networks, and everyone who comes into contact with you is a threat to an abuser. These people may see the bruises, they may ask you questions, they may encourage you to leave. You may start to think about prioritising the needs of your baby – as much as you want to keep your family unit together, you may recognise that this is not a good environment in which to bring your baby up. You may recognise the symptoms of anxiety or fear in your children and decide that enough is enough. You may recognise that you no longer recognise yourself.

We start to take the plunge by speaking out to someone who might help us, a professional, we confide in or a friend or family member when we break down in tears, we 'google' domestic abuse, or start imagining a different life. We aren't quite ready to leave yet, but we start to get stronger. We start mentally preparing ourselves, we know we will get out, it's just a matter of time, we start planning. Where will we go, where will we stay, how will we leave? One day – and sometimes when we least expect it, the moment arrives and we take the chance and leave.

"I always knew I would leave, it was just a matter of when. I tried a couple of times but he persuaded me to come back for the sake of the children. I struggled to cope with the children missing their dad. My worker told me to learn from this – don't see it as failing, learn from it, work out what went wrong last time and put things in place to make sure next time it was easier. The last time I left, I knew it was for good – I felt different, stronger. No matter what he said, my love for him had died. His words were scary but I just had to keep going. There was no way back for us."

Research shows that women leave an average of 8 times before they leave for good, so don't be too hard on yourself if it takes you more than one attempt. There are many reasons to stay, as well as many reasons to leave and only you will know when the time is right to leave for good. Try to be sure of your decision to leave before you do, as if you go back the abuse is often worse – after all you have left them once so they won't want to give you the opportunity again. They may be well behaved when you first return and again, they will promise you the world, but it is very unlikely to last and they will want to make sure you know exactly who is in charge again.

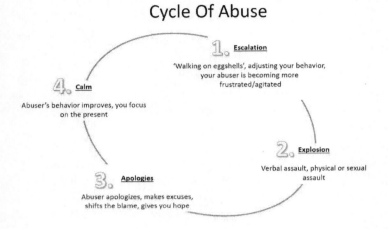

Cycle Of Abuse

1. Escalation
'Walking on eggshells', adjusting your behavior, your abuser is becoming more frustrated/agitated

2. Explosion
Verbal assault, physical or sexual assault

3. Apologies
Abuser apologizes, makes excuses, shifts the blame, gives you hope

4. Calm
Abuser's behavior improves, you focus on the present

If you are still struggling to make a decision, and you need a bit of reassurance about your decision to leave, look at this list of things people do when they are in happy, non-abusive relationships. The Happy Couples Checklist is at the back of the book.

Do you do any of these things with your partner?

What exactly are you fighting for?

Have confidence in your decision making and try to stick to it.

Complex Abusive Relationships

Sometimes these are labelled as 'toxic' relationships or 'co-dependent' relationships - where both parties seem to be as bad as each other. There may be a long history of arguments, physical abuse, screaming and shouting matches, police call-outs where both parties blame each other, yet refuse to break up.

In these relationships there are often underlying issues – drugs, alcohol dependency or mental health issues. Even without physical violence, these relationships are destructive. If you are addicted to drugs/alcohol, the abuser will encourage this – remember, they love you becoming dependent on them. If they know you are trying to drink less, they will encourage you to drink more, they will make you believe that it is impossible for you to drink less, so you feel like a failure. They will blame your mental health issues for their behaviour – threatening to report you to social care or to police. They know what your biggest fears are and they will use these against you.

They will use gaslighting techniques to make you believe the abuse is your fault. They will prevent you from getting help, they will make you believe you are 'just as bad as them'. They will tell you that nobody will believe you are being abused because you have abused them before. These relationships are very difficult to leave and over time as the abuse continues, your strength and will to leave will deteriorate further. Your dependency on drugs/alcohol will increase, your mental health will deteriorate.

Using alcohol or drugs as a way of coping with abuse is very common.

Did you know you are 9 times more likely to become dependent on alcohol if you are experiencing domestic abuse?

Many victims of abuse also experience some degree of depression or anxiety, panic attacks to PTSD (Post-Traumatic Stress Disorder) – after all, you are going through prolonged periods of intense stress so your 'stress bucket' is always full. You may even feel suicidal and feel like there is no escape, so the only way is to take your own life and put a stop to the hurting. This doesn't mean you have a mental illness. You are feeling this way because of your situation, because you are being abused. The way you feel is because of your situation.

It doesn't mean that you can't recover, you just need help to do it.

'' They tried to refer me to a programme for people with mental health issues and told me they were worried about what would happen to my children if I had a relapse. I am not mentally ill – I felt suicidal because of my ex. I lived with him for years, hearing threats to slit my throat or break my legs on a regular basis, like it had become normal to say that. Of course, I wasn't coping, I was terrified and had to find a way to survive, but it is different now, I am never going back and I feel like a different person now I am no longer with him.''

If you think this is you, get some professional help. They can help you discreetly without your partner knowing, they can help you explore ways of reducing your alcohol/drug intake or help you manage your mental health better whilst you prepare to leave your abuser.

There IS help available for you and you absolutely CAN recover!

How an abusive relationship affects you

As I have already said, you don't even notice at first that you are being abused – the silent drip feed of emotional abuse and control bring you down slowly. You may feel:

- Panicky for no specific reason, depressed, tearful

- Anxious when you have to explain something to your partner or anxious around other people. You may feel you have to check in with your partner about how you should behave

- You may worry about spending money, going out without your partner, about repercussions from your partner

- You may be forced to listen to your partner criticising you in front of others

- You may be forced to get pregnant or terminate a pregnancy even though you don't want this

- You may be forced to prioritise the needs of your partner over that of yourself and your children, even neglecting them because you are frightened of repercussions from your partner

- You may be accompanied all the time and never allowed any time on your own

- You may not be allowed to speak to other people, instead your partner may speak for you

- You may have to miss appointments or refuse help even though you want them

- You may lose interest in yourself and stop caring about your appearance or go overboard and clean excessively to hide the reality from others

- You may start drinking more alcohol, self-harm or take drugs to cope with the abuse

- You may cover up and make excuses to hide your injuries or your partner's behaviour

You may feel angry, frustrated, lash out at your abuser. This doesn't mean you are abusive – this means you are trying to be heard, trying to show them how much they are hurting you and wanting them to stop. This can be a dangerous time. It is like a bottle of fizzy pop being shaken and shaken, while the lid is still on - eventually it will explode. Don't let the bottle explode – seek help and get out. Don't struggle alone.

It won't get better and the way you feel won't get better until you take control back – yes, it is scary, but isn't living with your abuser scary too? The longer you are apart, the stronger you will become and the happier you will be.

CHAPTER 2:
ACTION

Services and Support

So, you feel brave, you have decided 'enough is enough' and you are ready to take action – now what do you do?

First of all, get some clarity on your options. Speak to a professional about what your best options are – should you stay in your own home, should you go to refuge, should you report to police, should you see a solicitor – these choices are all completely within your control and up to you. Every situation is different, just work out what you need to do first and do it.

In an emergency

If you are worried about your safety then the only people who can really help you are the police. Don't hesitate to call them – explain all your concerns, be open and honest, explain what help you want from them. When police attend any domestic abuse-related call-out they should make an automatic referral to your local domestic abuse organisation and social services if you have children or there are any other vulnerable people living in your home. Don't worry about this – the referral to the domestic abuse organisation is confidential so your ex won't be alerted. The police should speak to both parties individually, so be truthful and explain what has happened. This is your opportunity to let everything out – they can't help you if they don't know what is happening. Don't cover up for the abuse, don't make excuses, be honest. If your partner (ex) is arrested it is not your fault, it is his. Don't take on the responsibility for the consequences of his actions – if he hadn't been abusive then you wouldn't have had to call police, would you?

"My neighbours called police when they heard me screaming. When my ex opened the door, he told police we were just having an argument but I came to the door and they saw my bruised face and arrested him. He had slammed me into a door – it wasn't the first time, but it was the first time I had told anyone. I was furious at my neighbours to start off with but now I realise it was the best thing they could have done for me"

Social services

The social services referral is to alert them to the incident and the safeguarding concern- after all they are there to protect children. It doesn't mean they will come and take your children awa, all they want to know is that you are doing all you can to protect them. If this was the first incident where police were involved, if you are adamant you are ending the relationship and the social worker feels confident you will be able to protect the children in future, their intervention will probably stop after the initial assessment.

If you need support and help to protect your children, having them involved can also be a positive. It can allow you access to services that may not be available to you otherwise. If social services get involved with your case, they are there because they have significant concerns. It can be difficult and you can feel worried about their intervention and feel like you have to defend your parenting decisions but don't battle against them, work with them.

Show them how you will protect your children, agree to any support they may offer you who doesn't need a bit of parenting guidance?! If you don't feel like the professionals are hearing you or understanding your situation, invite an IDVA to support you in safeguarding meetings. This will help you feel more supported and they can speak up on your behalf if they have any concerns.

"I really didn't want social services involved but actually it was the best thing that could have happened. They told my ex he wasn't allowed to see the children until he had completed a perpetrator programme. He said he wouldn't, so now he isn't allowed to see them. They also sent me to the Freedom Programme which opened my eyes to the different tactics of abuse, which I couldn't see at the time."

IDVA Support

Having an IDVA (Independent Domestic Violence Advocate) is your best ally when separating from an abusive ex. They are the experts on supporting people experiencing all forms of abuse and controlling behaviour. They are independent and they are focussed on YOU. They will speak up on your behalf, they will challenge professionals where needed and they will explain all the options to you and work through a collaborative support plan to help you work things through.

Safety always has to be the priority so they will create a really comprehensive safety plan with you and then work out an action plan step by step. They will help you understand and navigate the professional processes if you are going through court or involved with child protection proceedings.

If there is one professional you want on your side through everything it is an IDVA - they are passionate about protecting people experiencing domestic abuse, with knowledge and contacts to help you with everything from organising screens at court, professionals' meetings to hear your case, sourcing video doorbells and safety measures, to sourcing grants for washing machines when yours decides to blow up in the middle of all of the chaos! I cannot recommend IDVA support enough – and best of all, their support is absolutely free! Contact your local domestic abuse organisation for support.

"My IDVA was my angel. She called me at least twice a week, she found me a solicitor, she referred my children into their children's team so they could get the support they needed. She came with me to every child protection meeting and made sure that everyone who could help me, did. It was so lovely to think she cared so much about my family."

Refuge

Refuges are usually homes consisting of shared accommodation where you have your own bedroom but share the bathrooms and living facilities. The refuges usually just look like 'normal' houses or flats. There is a national database of refuge vacancies so that any IDVA service can see which spaces are available, should someone need to flee from in a hurry. You won't get a choice of where you go, it just depends on the space available to suit your needs, but you can of course always move again when another space becomes available.

You will have to give up work to go to refuge and your children will have to leave school. It can seem like a lot to give up, having to leave your home, family, friends, behind but remember this is not forever and children are resilient so they will adjust to moving school. Don't stay at home just because you don't want to give that up - if you are at risk, furniture can be replaced, you can't! Safety has to come above everything, so if you need to go to refuge, just go!

The address has to remain confidential for your safety and that of the other families in refuge. If you disclose the address the staff will have no option but to move you on. You can keep in touch with safe family and friends and meet them at a safe, neutral location (not your home area) but you cannot tell them where you live. There will be some rules in place in the refuge to keep you safe, but it is not a prison and you will have the time, space and the specialist help you and your children need to recover.

"I was so scared going to refuge as I had no idea what it would be like. It took a little while to settle in but it was so nice not having to feel scared any more. The staff helped me with my son as his behaviour got really bad once we were in refuge – it was like he was letting it all out. It was nice to have support from the other mums too – they understood. The staff are helping me think about what I want to do in future now. I want to start my own business so they have found me a course and are providing the childcare so I can attend."

Of course, if you don't think refuge is for you and you choose to stay home, an IDVA can still help you through outreach support or you could find a specialist divorce coach like me! The important thing is that you don't try and struggle through this alone.

Housing

Local authority housing departments have a duty of care now to provide accommodation for victims of domestic abuse if they are in priority need ie vulnerable due to pregnancy, if you have children in your care, or you are a care leaver under 21 years of age. The criteria will be widened for all victims of domestic abuse when the new DA Bill comes in, in 2021. It is always worth seeking advice from your local authority housing options team or your housing association to see what help they can give you when considering separation from your abuser as the support they can offer you varies from case to case, by organisation and by geographical area.

As with any professional meeting, take someone with you if you can, so you can make notes to refer to afterwards.

Voluntary organisations

There are loads of these around! Everything from organisations who will offer a befriending service for isolated people, single parents and the vulnerable to specialist drugs and alcohol organisations. If you need to improve your skills so you can become financially independent there will be an organisation that can help you. If you need help to manage debts as a result of economic abuse, organisations like Step Change and Money Advice Plus can help you. Don't think that you have to navigate this journey alone – you don't. If you have support from others – even just a little bit of support, it can help you feel stronger. The people supporting you can keep you motivated and you will feel more confident about seeing it through to the end. There is a list of resources at the back of this book to get you started.

''*My local Home-Start organisation provided a befriender for me. My abuser had isolated me from all my friends and family so I was struggling with 2 children and one who had behavioural difficulties. Just knowing she was coming round each week helped me feel stronger. She would take the children out to give me a break or sit and play with them so I could catch up on some sleep or make dinner. It was such a help!*''

Health Services

Talk to your GP as a first point of call. Do you need to take some time off work to give yourself a break? Do you need a referral to Talking Therapies or is there some other kind of support they could link you up to? If you have young children, could your Health visitor provide more support for you? Get as much support around you as possible. Create a great support team and you will feel a whole lot stronger.

Prepare to Exit

Why don't you just leave?? If I had a £ for every time I heard that I would be a millionaire! If it was that easy there would be no need for domestic abuse services or refuges who are overwhelmed with women seeking help in a crisis. We wait until things get so bad for us that we have no option but to seek help. We are only just starting to talk about abuse in relationships – schools thankfully now have domestic abuse on the curriculum, but certainly when I was in school or with my friends, we never talked about what was ok and what wasn't. I wouldn't have known a ''boundary' if it had jumped up and smacked me in the face!

We don't recognise abuse because we have never been taught how to recognise it, we don't speak about it, because our abuser has told us not to and we have no idea what help there is available even when we try to reach out. We feel guilty we didn't leave sooner or that we didn't spot the signs, but how would we know if nobody ever told us what to look for? I have already said that the abuse doesn't start on 'day 1' of your relationship – it seeps in slowly, you can't see it and by the time you do see it, it's almost too late – almost.

Leaving can seem too difficult. We can make excuses too, justify our actions, (or lack of), resolve to try harder, to give him another chance, to put off leaving by giving ourselves a deadline– then move that deadline further and further away. ''Maybe when the kids leave school'', ''maybe once he gets a different job there will be less pressure on him'', ''let's just get Christmas done and then see what happens''. Before you know it, years have passed and we are still stuck in the same situation. Actually, it can be worse, because by staying we are effectively giving the abuser permission to abuse us – we don't leave, so therefore we make it acceptable for our abuser to abuse.

''I used to sit every Christmas thinking to myself – next year it won't be like this. I didn't want another Christmas where I felt so miserable, but yet here I am again. I don't know what

is stopping me leaving. He has no relationship with the kids, we don't spend any time together as a family, we are all miserable, yet I stay."

'...but he's a good dad' – another common phrase that victims often say and another excuse to stay when leaving can seem too difficult. No good dad would let his children experience domestic abuse. The impact of domestic abuse on children is well documented – they hear things, they see things, no matter how much you try and protect them and want to believe yours are different. If you believe staying in an abusive relationship is better than breaking up the family you are wrong – but also remember you are not the one breaking it up. If your abuser didn't behave in that way there would be no reason to break up the family, so who should feel the burden of responsibility? Not you!

"I couldn't think straight – it was like my head was full of cotton wool. He used to say I was stupid because I couldn't remember things, but this was because I was exhausted mentally. So much had happened too, I forgot things and only remembered them once I had left. I learnt to write things down and always took someone with me to meetings so they could focus for me if I was struggling. Gradually the fog cleared."

Each time you leave, you are testing the water – am I able to cope on my own? Is he going to report me to social care like he said he would? Am I going to be believed when I tell people? Of course, each time you leave, there are a million reasons to leave and a million reasons to stay too. Hurdles such as having to leave your home, take your children out of school, financial worries and lack of support can all make it easier to stay with your abusive partner.

Unfortunately, domestic abuse services in the UK suffer through lack of funding and it can be a postcode lottery as to the support you can receive when you do reach out for help. This is why knowing your options before you leave is important, as is educating yourself on the tactics of abuse, so you can recognise the 'game playing' and protect yourself- these are all essential skills vital to your recovery. The only person you can rely on to make a change to this situation is you – but get your plans in place first, get stronger and you can do it!

First things first – PLEASE, PLEASE, PLEASE if you are considering leaving your abusive partner, plan it if you can and get advice and help with planning your exit.

2 women die every week in the UK due to domestic abuse.

In this book I will be talking about abusers being men. I have supported male victims of abuse too, but the reality is that women are much more likely to be the victims of domestic abuse and the evidence overwhelmingly shows that women are more likely to be killed. Fact.

Don't get lulled into a false sense of security if your relationship is not physically abusive. In many cases where women are murdered by their partner or ex-partner there is very little, if any, physical violence in the lead up to it. The physical abuse often starts when the abuser fears they are losing control – often during pregnancy (because they are no longer no.1 priority for you) or separation. The most dangerous time for a victim is the first 3 months after leaving, so don't think once you have walked out the front door you are safe.

Please don't assume 'it will never happen to me' or assume that because the abuse isn't physical that it is not dangerous – things can change in a split second. This is all scary stuff to think about, but it's much better to be aware of the risks, forewarned and forearmed, and to manage the risks by using the tools and the strategies in this book than go ahead blindly, keeping your fingers crossed that everything will be ok.

You may have no choice but to leave – you may have to leave in a hurry because it is too dangerous for you to stay any longer or because you have been told to leave by police or social care in order to protect yourself and your children. This is the most difficult position to be in because the rush causes panic and you may not have a choice. If you also haven't worked out whether you want to end the relationship or not yet, going to refuge isn't really going to be suitable. You will feel isolated, you may still communicate with your partner and will be easily persuaded back again. Your abuser will be scared this will happen again and put more control measures in place, making life more unbearable than it was before.

You really don't want to be forced to leave to go to refuge – you won't get a choice of where that is, so you could literally be hundreds of miles away from your friends and family and will have to give up everything to go. Of course, if going to refuge IS your choice, then the staff there will support you 100% to help you settle and make a fresh start. Much better to get the help and support you need sooner, before it becomes a crisis. Much better that you decide which option works better for you – going to refuge completely out of area to make a fresh start or staying put at home with protective orders and a robust safety and support plan in place.

Wherever possible, the choice should be yours – it's important you start to have some choice over your life and regain control.

Preparation and planning

The worst thing you can do is tell a controlling partner you are leaving - everything they do relates to having total power and control over the person they abuse - so to know that they are losing that control is devastating to them and they will do whatever they can to regain that control.

For obvious reasons I am not going to bullet point all the preparation tips for leaving an abusive relationship – for one thing I don't want to give any potential perpetrators the 'heads up' and for another this has to be planned appropriately for the individual. You know your partner and you know the best time to leave and the help you need. Get professional advice from your local IDVA (Independent Domestic Violence Advocate) based in your local Women's Aid or domestic abuse service. Google domestic abuse in your area or look on local Council pages and a contact number should come up. Their advice is free, confidential and it could save your life.

If you ask for help and you get turned away or told that you can't get the help you need, please don't give up. Unfortunately, because of the way lots of statutory and voluntary services are funded these days and because many of them have strict funding criteria, they may not be able to help you straight away. Keep asking, keep shouting for the help you need until you get it. Don't give up! If one organisation can't help you, go somewhere else. Talk to your GP, to your Health Visitor, to a trusted friend or family member or call a helpline like the National Domestic Violence Helpline, which is free and open 24 hours a day.

Find out your Rights when it comes to your housing, finances, the children and the future. You may well find that all the things you have been threatened with are not in actual fact, correct at all. These lies are designed to keep you in the relationship. You may well be entitled to more financially than you imagined. Even if you aren't, is it worth staying just for the sake of your financial future? Yes, you may have to sell the house and move to a smaller property or even have to stay in rented or temporary accommodation until you get back on your feet – but remember this is only short-term.

The more clarity you can get on your options, the possibilities and choices you might have when you leave, the more confident you will feel about making that choice. Most professionals offer free initial advice, so it doesn't even cost you anything at this point. Find out the information first then you can start to make decisions for your future. Open your mind to possibilities:

What might it be like to live nearer to your family?

Can you consider renting somewhere just to pause until things settle?

What support could you get for the children to help them adjust?

Could you stay in your home while you separate?

Who could be in your support team?

What plans can you put in place to make your exit as easy and as safe as possible?

"He persuaded me to stay, saying he was under pressure at work and that was why he was so stressed. I asked him to go to therapy, he refused. He told me it was my fault he was unhappy. He still criticised me in front of the kids, he put zero effort into changing his behaviour even when he knew it was crunch time, so that was it. I was done. ''

What if you can't leave?

Leaving your home may not be an option immediately. You may not be able to afford to leave your home or you may be tied to a joint tenancy with your abuser. Use this time to get yourself stronger, start planning for life after you move out and use good coping strategies to make sure that their behaviour affects you less.

If an incident happens and you need to call police but want to remain at home, the police may be able to issue a DAPN (Domestic Abuse Protection Notice) to keep your partner away from your home for up to 28 days. The police, the Council or your Housing Association may be able to put extra safety measures in place at home for you. You can get outreach support from your local domestic abuse service. You may also be able to apply for an injunction (Non-Molestation Order) to give you some legal protection from your ex. There ARE options.

Work out ways to keep some physical distance between you.

Can you sleep in another room?

Can you make excuses to limit the time you spend together?

Can you let the criticisms and the jibes go?

Try and keep the situation as calm as it can be. You just need to get through this with as little stress and conflict as possible. Keep focussed – it won't always be this way - you have just got to grit your teeth and get through it. Walk away, go out for a walk, go to bed early. Spend more time with friends re-connecting, start 'squirreling' some of your money away discreetly so you have some when you need it, start to build up a support network ready for when you do leave. Start researching, do things that help you cope better and feel stronger and remember each day is a day nearer to the time when your new life can begin.

When I left for the final time after 2 previous failed attempts, I knew what to expect- the tears, the begging not to break up the family, the promises to change. I had seen and heard them a million times before, I could almost recite them word for word! So predictable!

By the 3rd attempt I knew I had had enough. I was exhausted mentally and physically and knew this had to stop. I had my lightbulb moment. I knew I wasn't going back this time. I just knew it – this time it was different. I felt different. I felt stronger, I felt angry at the way I was being treated. The anger turned to resentment and helped me feel stronger. Everything he usually did that affected me didn't work anymore, the love had completely disappeared and it was like I was living with a stranger. I knew I deserved better, so I put my plans in place. I was strong on the outside but quivering on the inside.

I asked my friend to find out how much train tickets cost, no need to explain – she guessed why I needed them. I knew I had to put distance between us or else he would do as he had done before and talk 'at me' till the early hours, trying to convince me of all the reasons I should return until I was so exhausted, I would agree just to shut him up.

It didn't exactly go to plan (Sod's Law!). He had obviously sussed something was going on and provoked an argument so he was late going to work – they have a sixth sense I swear! My friend had to drive round and round the block waiting for him to leave. We quickly threw some stuff into a suitcase, then she drove me to the station and put me on the train with both of us sobbing and me shaking like a leaf – the passengers must have wondered what on earth was going on! I had taken the first step – there was no going back this time.

Here are some tips for you when preparing to leave:

* **Confide** in a trusted friend or family member about your plans. If you tell someone else then it's happening right? Telling someone makes it real, gives you more motivation to carry it through and keeps you feeling strong enough to do it. Be careful that this person won't let 'the cat out of the bag' and definitely don't tell children in advance. Not only does this put too much emotional pressure on them, but the less they know, the better – they can't slip up, and they will ultimately be much safer if they don't know anything about your plans.

* **Act normal**. Keep things calm if you can to get to 'D' day. Try and keep to your usual routines. You don't want to raise any suspicion. Keep focussed.

* **Put some distance between you**. Try and get some physical distance between you if you can. You may not be able to or want to leave your home, but if you can then this physical distance can help you stay stronger in those early days. If you need to go to a refuge, the domestic abuse organisation will work out a plan to get you there. Don't see this as a 'forever' home – simply a stop-gap to help you recover. If you can stay with friends/family that are supportive, that can also help, but don't be upset if they don't want to get involved – it can be scary for them too and they may be worried about repercussions from your ex.

*Don't leave evidence lying around. Keep anything that might arouse suspicion out of the house if possible. Abusers have a 'sixth sense' and they will snoop and try and find evidence if they suspect you may be getting support or leaving.

* **Plan in advance** as much as you can for your exit. Imagine how things are going to go and then prepare a back-up 'Plan B', so you have most if not all eventualities covered.

If you can't stay at your parent's could you stay at a friend's?

What if he doesn't go to work on time?

What if he takes the car so I don't have any transport?

What if I can't take everything that I need with me?

Try and consider all the different scenarios that could possibly happen and what you would do to overcome them – this way you will have it all covered.

Plan – Try and set yourself a deadline and a good day/time when it might be easiest to leave.

Plan - For every possible scenario – if he doesn't go to work on time how will that affect your plans? Can you adapt your plan?

Plan – Where will you go – do you need to tell them in advance or can you just turn up?

Plan – Do you need help to get to somewhere safe – who do you need to help you?

Plan – How will you get the children, what do you need to take with you?

Plan – If you left before and went back, why was that? What can you do differently this time to make sure that doesn't happen again?

Plan – But if you need to leave sooner because you feel too unsafe, then do. Don't wait.

"The trouble is you think you have time" – Buddha

Here's a list of items you may wish to take with you:

- Originals or copies of marriage/divorce certificate, birth certificates, financial documents, bank statements, benefits letters, passports, Visa documents, mortgage documents

- Baby milk, bottles, nappies, changes of clothes, soothers, favourite toy

- Bank and credit cards

- Car keys, house keys, cash

- Medical cards/ prescription medication

- Court documents

- Mobile phone and charger with numbers for professionals supporting you

Take the most important items with you and anything particularly sentimental that you can carry, and don't worry if you can't get the rest. The most important thing is that you get out safely – everything else can be sorted later. If you have to leave certain things behind, leave them – remember it is just 'stuff'. 'Stuff' can be replaced – you can't be replaced..

No regrets

You may think you aren't strong enough to leave the relationship– but staying is often more exhausting than leaving. Once you have left, you don't have to live with them criticising and scrutinising your every move, you have space to breathe to think, to sleep, to recuperate and get stronger. Imagine what that could be like? To wake up with the sound of silence, peace, calm.

"I love waking up each morning now – nobody shouting at me, telling me off for spending too long in the shower. Now I spend as long as I want in there, just because I can!"

You might believe you are able to protect the children from the abuse, but children see and hear more than you think and it does affect them, no matter how much you don't want to believe that. All the research shows children are hugely affected by living with domestic abuse – they are much more likely to suffer from long-term mental health problems, more likely to repeat the same behaviour as adults, more likely to be hurt physically by their abuser.

Don't think your children are ok through all of this – they are not. Even the youngest children pick up on abusive behaviour. Protect your children, be strong and end this relationship as soon as it is safe to do so.

"I thought my children were asleep when incidents happened, but in therapy my son drew a picture of me being held under the water by his dad. My daughter told her teacher she had seen 'daddy throw mummy over the table'. It shocked me to know that they had seen and heard way more than I thought they had."

Your abuser will use every reason under the sun to try and persuade you to stay. They will sob, plead, cry, bully, threaten, do anything they can to try and persuade you to stay or to reconcile. You will have to stay tough to get through this part. I often talk about letting their words wash over you like a wave, not letting them soak through your skin. These words are tactics designed to get you back home 'where you belong'.

DON'T believe them – remember why you wanted to leave in the first place. Focus on what life could be like in the future without them and their rules. Don't give in. I know it isn't easy and it can often seem easier to go back home, but you don't want to have any regrets. It definitely isn't easy when you first leave, I can't sugar-coat it, it is tough, but the longer you stay away and the more distance you have from your ex, the stronger you will become. This will become your new 'normal'.

Breathe.

Remember all the big decisions about your long-term future such as where you are going to live, how you are going to manage financially, how you are going to work out child contact etc, can be sorted out as time goes on. The most important thing is that you get out, THAT IS IT. Your mind can get carried away and before you know it you have played out your life over the next 10 years and you become completely overwhelmed. Think 'one step at a time' – don't think about the next 10 years, focus on moment to moment. Bring yourself back to now.

Court Orders and legal protection

You may be ready to end your relationship and wondering how you are going to do that if your abuser refuses to leave the home. Why should you give up your home, your support network, your job, everything that is familiar to you? The good news is for many people experiencing domestic abuse you don't actually have to. There are lots of safety measures that can be put in place to make your home physically safer – alarms, alerts that notify police of potential danger, special security locks, etc. When considering whether to leave your home or not, consider your options.

There are Court Orders (in the UK) that can be applied for by police or by you to protect you and your children:

Domestic Abuse Protection Orders

Applied for by police when they attend an incident and believe there has been an incident of domestic abuse, yet there is insufficient evidence at that point to charge the alleged perpetrator with a criminal offence. These are sometimes referred to as DVPN's (Domestic Violence Protection Orders) but will change to DAPO's in 2021. Police don't need the victim's consent and this order means that the perpetrator has to stay away from you and from the property for up to 28 days. This allows you time to get any practical help and advice you need and allows you some 'headspace' so you think more clearly about what you want to do. You may be able to change the locks, you may have time to seek an injunction against your abuser, you have time to think about whether this is really the kind of relationship you want to be in. It gives you space to breathe, to consider your options.

Clare's Law

You can ask police confidentially for information on your partner's history and direct family members such as your parents can also ask. If you are separated from your ex you won't be entitled to a Clare's law disclosure, but sometimes this knowledge can be can be influential in decision-making about whether to remain with your partner or not. Please be mindful though that getting this information can take a while and the information they give you is only related to domestic abuse criminal offences. If it comes back clear it is no guarantee your partner is safe, it may just be that they were never reported to police. Trust your gut instinct. If something is telling you it feels wrong, it probably is.

" My boyfriend told me that he wasn't allowed to see his kids because his ex was a bitch and just jealous. I found out after making a Clare's Law application that she actually has a Restraining Order against him and his previous partners had also reported him to police. What a liar!"

Injunctions (Non-Molestation Orders)

- These can be applied for in an emergency without alerting your abuser

- There usually has to have been an incident of assault within the previous 2 weeks or you can apply under special circumstances and recount a pattern of abusive behaviour to show why you need an emergency order

- You will probably have to pay for this application as Legal Aid is very restricted at present

- Consider whether this order is likely to increase your risk or decrease it depending on how your abuser is likely to react

- This is your legal protection, keep a copy on you at all times

- This order may last up to 6 months and mean that your abuser can't contact you, attend your address and restrictions can also include being unable to contact you through other people or social media

- The abuser may be told to contact you via a solicitor with regards to child contact

- The order is a criminal order if breached – the responsibility is yours to report any breaches to police

- There will be a return hearing where your abuser can state his objections, but you can have screens at court, wait in a separate area and have your legal representative with you to speak on your behalf

Occupation Orders

- An order to remove one party from the home when a joint tenancy or joint mortgage

- Often applied for at the same time as an NMO

- Can be difficult to obtain if your abuser doesn't have anywhere else to go or can't afford to move out

- Can state the rules as to how both parties live together in the home until the home is sold or divorce and financial proceedings are concluded.

Criminal Charges

- There is no specific criminal offence for domestic abuse. An abuser has to be charged with a specific offence such as assault, harassment, stalking or Actual Bodily Harm. There IS a specific offence for coercive control.

- The responsibility for charging does not fall on your shoulders –this is for the police and the CPS (Crown Prosecution Service) to decide. The CPS can also decide to go ahead with the prosecution even if you withdraw your statement.

- You can request a Restraining order, and in some cases, this can be granted even if the abuser is found not guilty. A Restraining Order is the criminal law equivalent of a NMO and can often be granted for a long period of time, sometimes indefinitely.

Preparing for Criminal Court

- You don't need a solicitor – you are not the person on trial, you are a witness. The CPS is effectively your solicitor, to put forward your side of the story in court.

- The first step is a plea hearing – you won't have to attend this hearing. This is when the abuser goes to Magistrates Court to enter their plea of 'guilty' or 'not guilty'. If they plead 'not guilty' the case will be adjourned to a trial, either in Magistrates Court or at Crown Court. This will then be your opportunity to attend and give evidence.

- If the abuser pleads 'guilty', sentencing may be adjourned while a pre-Sentence Report is completed by probation. A probation officer will interview the abuser to gain some understanding of the abuser's insight into his behaviour, any vulnerabilities, potential risk to the victim or others in future and they will make a recommendation on sentencing to the court.

- Make sure you give everything that could help to police – they may request evidence of emails, they may wish to download information from your mobile phone, they may request photographs, they may obtain medical evidence from your GP or hospital.

- You will be asked to complete a Victim Personal Statement (VPS) prior to court and you may be asked to do this a couple of times – this is because how you feel a few months before court and how you feel immediately before can be quite different.

- The VPS is your opportunity to explain to court how this incident has affected you. You will be given some guidance on what to include in this, but it can include how it has affected you emotionally, financially, socially.

- You can have a pre-trial visit to see the court room and stand in the witness box before the trial, to prepare you for the day.

- You will be given a separate waiting room from your abuser and Victim Service/Support will often arrange for one of their team to sit with you and support you on the day.

- Many defendants choose to plead not guilty in the hope that the victim won't give evidence - they may also choose for their case to be heard at Crown Court in the hope that a jury of laypeople will be more sympathetic, so don't be surprised if that happens.

- Don't be surprised if the charges get reduced from a more serious offence to a lesser one. It can often seem better to ensure a conviction for a lesser offence than risk a 'not guilty' conclusion for a more serious offence.

- Be vigilant in the lead up to trial as your abuser may try and persuade you against giving evidence – they may start to contact you again, plead with you, persuade you, harass you. Remember they know how to manipulate you – if this happens it is important that you report this to police so they can manage this and protect you.

- Don't feel guilty if your abuser gets arrested or convicted of an offence – the outcome is not determined by you. If your abuser hadn't been abusive in the first place, they wouldn't have set the balls in motion.

- Remember how scared you must have felt at the time. Did they care how you felt then????

Preparing for Civil Court (Family Court or County Court)

- You can represent yourself (Litigant in Person) – not recommended if going up against an ex with a controlling personality

- You can hire a Divorce Consultant – someone who is legally trained and can help you prepare statements and casework prior to court but doesn't represent you in person at hearings

- You can hire a McKenzie Friend - a professional who has legal knowledge and can provide emotional support, sit with you in court and take notes to help you.

- You can hire a Family Law Solicitor who may also need to instruct a barrister for some of the proceedings

- You can hire a direct access barrister – you can instruct a barrister without the need for a solicitor

- Do your research – find out how much each option is likely to cost you and try to understand the process. Make sure whichever professional you choose, that they have plenty of experience dealing with domestic abuse cases. This is much more important than the price – they need to be able to recognise the tactics, predict the abuser's next move and have a good, adaptable strategy to support you and try and win your case.

- Evidence, evidence, evidence! Courts look at facts rather than opinions so make sure you keep a log of texts/emails/threats/photos of injuries etc from your ex. Keep it organised – get yourself a filing system as you may need to refer back to things in future.

- Try and communicate wherever possible by email or text with your ex and your legal team so you have a trail.

- If your hearing is virtual you can still ask not to see your ex on screen if you have evidence of domestic abuse or if it is in person you can request screens or video link (where available).

- Remember your case will progress and what started out as a simple case can soon turn into a more complex one, so take it one step at a time and weight up your options as you go.

"I had no idea how brutal the court hearings would be - everything was scrutinised. Your whole family is under the spotlight. They spoke to the children and to me and my ex would not budge on what he wanted. He wasn't thinking about how it would impact on them at all, it was all about what suited him. It took a year of hearings before we finally got the Child Arrangement Order."

For all court cases

- Get to court in plenty of time – request a separate waiting room if available.

- Take a hot drink and snacks with you as it can be a long day. Court cases rarely run to schedule - the allocated time often runs over. Make sure you put enough money in the parking meter or better still pay by phone so you can pay at the end of the day.

- Make sure your mobile is charged and on silent when the court hearing is happening.

- Always take someone with you for support. No matter how strong and independent you want to be, it is always a good idea to have someone with you.

- Dress like 'you on your best day' – this will give you the confidence you need. Have your shoulders back, head high. Don't worry if you get upset – it shows you are human. Don't worry if you can't remember something – be honest, open, clear and concise.

- Be prepared to hear lies and mistruths from the other side – make a note if you can and speak to your legal representative about how to challenge it.

- Wear something to remind you of who you are – a bracelet with special meaning or a ring with an engraving or a simple fidget toy/stress ball. Look or fidget with this when you get stressed or upset or when you need reassurance.

- Don't be surprised if your ex gets angry or tries to interrupt and control proceedings – they will want to intimidate you. You may hear lots of huffing and puffing or notice them staring at you. Remember you are protected in court, they can't hurt you. Stay strong and focussed, don't let their behaviour distract you. You aren't alone.

- Wait for a while at the end of your hearing to have a debrief with your representative and let your ex leave court.

- Don't ruminate over what happened earlier in the day – it's done, you can't change it. Take some time to gather yourself, do something nice to shake it off and then think about what your next step is.

- Keep a copy of any injunction / Restraining Order on you at all times in case an incident happens and you need to call 999.

"I was shaking like a leaf when I went to court but my IDVA came with me and she was amazing. She explained everything as it happened – she organised a separate

waiting area, she escorted me to the toilet and on breaks to make sure I never bumped into him. He lied in court but I was able to stay calm and I felt stronger as the day went on. I am glad I went through with it now — I don't feel sorry for him anymore."

Divorcing a controlling ex

Don't for goodness sake, choose a solicitor based on your best friend's experience. Her case may have been very different to yours and just because she liked them, doesn't mean you will. You have to have trust in your solicitor, you have to connect emotionally with them at some level too — you have to know they 'have your back'.

- Always speak to at least two or three different solicitors before you commit.

- If your ex is controlling and abusive, you might not want to waste your time thinking about collaborative law (where solicitors try and come to an amicable arrangement without the use of Courts). This works really well when you have couples who are willing to mediate, but your ex is highly unlikely to do so, so it is highly unlikely to work and you may just experience more stress, give him more opportunities to emotionally abuse you and it will cost you money for the pleasure of it!

- Most people who experience abusive relationships divorce their ex under the category of unreasonable behaviour. You will have to detail at least 5 different ways in which you believe your ex fits this category. Your ex will see this detail, so be mindful of how they might react. You may want to choose some points which are less likely to be antagonistic.

- Alternatively, the 2 - year separation rule may be an option for you or even the new 'no blame' category which is coming in later in 2021 if using unreasonable behaviour feels too daunting. To be honest, when you get your Decree Absolute (the final divorce paper) it doesn't say on there what the category is anyway. Make it as easy for yourself as you can.

- Don't spend money arguing over the divorce – it really doesn't matter in the grand scheme of things. You just want to get it done as quickly and easily as possible.

- Always get specialist advice around your finances and what you might be entitled to in future before you tick or untick the box about financial proceedings on your divorce application. Don't make decisions on finances without speaking to a specialist – you could be doing yourself out of money further down the line.

- If you are going to mediate over financial proceedings, pick your battles– don't argue over the small things, let them go and move on. You want to extract yourself from your ex as quickly as possible so don't waste time and energy fighting over the small stuff, it's really not worth it.

- Always, always get legal advice – don't do the divorce on your own if you are going up against a controlling ex. Practically all family law solicitors offer a free initial consultation so make use of it. The very nature of a controlling ex will make sure that they try and bully you into agreeing to stuff, they will try and persuade you that their offer is the best one for you, they will threaten to drag you through the courts and cut you off without a penny, as they hide money and lie to win. They love winning!

- Build yourself a support team – a solicitor, a financial advisor and a coach as well as friends/family to help you through this process. No matter what they say at the beginning, the ex WILL make it difficult, because as with everything else, this is all about control.

"My ex keeps offering to talk it through over lunch, so we can come to an agreement without using lawyers. I know it is because he wants to railroad me into agreeing to what he wants. I have told him I am not prepared to discuss things in person with him and it will have to be discussed in mediation. He doesn't like that I am standing up to him now and it makes me really anxious but I feel more in control now."

- Keep reminding yourself that although this journey is hard, it WILL end. You don't have to be tied to your ex forever. You can even start using your maiden name before the divorce is finalised! Doing this helps you reclaim your identity. Bank accounts, utilities, benefits and passport changes can come after you receive your Absolute - and what a great feeling it is when you do that!

- Try and have as much control over proceedings as possible. It may seem like a good idea for your ex to pay for everything when you are married, but when you separate, what happens then? Can you change the utilities into your name? What happens if you want to move house and they are still on the tenancy? What does the maintenance money cover? Does it include costs of school uniforms, holidays, school trips? Try and work out the detail as much as possible, so you are really clear on what you are agreeing to.

- There can be all sorts of tax and pension implications when you divorce. Don't just think about the short-term, get good advice so you can understand what your longer-term financial future looks like. Many financial advisors don't charge at the beginning of the proceedings – their fee comes out of the settlement, so it is in their interest to get the best settlement for you.

- Remember, your solicitor is not your friend. They are working for you – if you aren't happy with their advice, say so. Change your solicitor if you aren't happy.

- Don't call your legal representative to offload – you can use a Divorce Coach or a friend for this. You will get better advice and it will certainly be a lot cheaper than a call to your solicitor.

- Make sure your legal representative gives you realistic expectations as you go about costs and outcomes as things can change from hearing to hearing and costs can quickly escalate. Will their fee be fixed and if so when does the fixed fee end if things are becoming protracted and lengthy? Are there things you can do yourself to reduce costs? Do you need to be clear on how you, your solicitor and your ex communicate? Do you need to instruct your solicitor not to respond to your ex unless you authorise it? I have known many an ex rack up a legal bill for their victim by harassing the opposing solicitor.

- Take control, but be realistic. Court proceedings are never simple when there is one controlling party. Proceedings are unlikely to be resolved within one hearing or one mediation sitting. Be prepared to have several meetings/court hearings until things are concluded.

"It was a bit of a battle. He wasn't happy that I got more than a 50/50 split. He was pushing for more time with the children for financial reasons, as that would have reduced his maintenance payments and his behaviour got worse in the lead up to the house being sold. Today I finally received my Absolute. I could have done a happy dance! I am finally free of him!"

Co-habiting couples

As above, make sure you get legal advice. There is no such thing as 'common-law' spouse these days, so don't assume that because you have been in a relationship for a significant time or contributed to the mortgage, that you will be entitled to an equal share. You have far fewer rights than if you are married.

In either case, married or not, you should also get advice on Wills and finances to ensure you are aware of all of the implications and to protect your financial future.

Mediation

- If you have evidence from police, health services or your domestic abuse organisation, of domestic abuse or child abuse, then you can submit this to court via a C100 form, who will take this into consideration so you may be exempt from mediation.

- If you don't have such evidence you will be invited to an individual MIAM (Mediation Information and Assessment Meeting). The mediator will see you and your ex separately and complete an assessment to determine whether mediation will be suitable for you or not. If not, they will submit their report to court explaining the reasons why.

- Even when there has been a history of domestic abuse, mediation can still be possible. You can do shuttle mediation where you don't sit with your ex, but the mediator shuttles back and forth between you. Mediation is an opportunity for you to put forward your suggestions as to how the child contact and co-parenting may work as you go forwards and also to mediate around a financial settlement.

- Be open-minded, go in there open to possibilities. Have a list of points you are not willing to budge on, those you might and those that you aren't really too concerned about at all.

- Think about how parenting agreements may work long-term not just short-term. Keep it child-focussed, what will work for the children?

- Try to accept you are unlikely to get it all your way — what would be the best-case scenario for you?

- Don't be bullied into agreeing anything that you are really not happy about. If you are adamant you don't want to agree to something, think about why that is. Can you do some research to get a bit more clarity on this issue? Sometimes change is scary at first and we say no because we feel out of control, but once we have more clarity the original issue becomes more viable.

- Make notes in the meeting so you can refer to them afterwards. You don't have to agree everything in the meeting — you can go away, find out more information, have a think about it and come back to the next meeting with your thoughts and proposals.

- It can be useful to use a parenting agreement template to help guide you through the issues you might need to agree on.

- You should have the Form E financial disclosure form to help you understand your ex's financial status and to help you work out what might be a fair settlement. Make sure you get legal advice from a solicitor or financial advisor on this before agreeing anything.

- The meetings usually last a couple of hours, make sure you have a drink with you. You can ask for a break at any time.

- Mediation can help you keep your case out of court, so you may have more control over what happens with the children than if your case goes before a judge. It can also be much cheaper than going to court and the agreement can be legally binding.

- Mediators are impartial and well used to dealing with controlling ex's, so they should make sure that you are protected. If you feel vulnerable, they will try and help you through it, but if it is just too difficult, then you can stop.

- Some solicitors will advise you not to bother with mediation if your ex is very controlling, as they are unlikely to want to mediate at all. This can be very true – after all, they thrive on control, so why would they want to give any of that up to you? However, some people want to try mediation to prove to themselves that they have given it a go and tried their best to resolve the issues before it goes to court. Take it one step at a time and do what feels right for you.

Safety Planning

If the police are involved, they will go through a safety plan with you and similarly so an IDVA or a specialist Divorce Coach will too.

How safe is your home?

You can buy devices online for a few pounds that can help you feel safer in your own home – window locks, door alarms, door jammers that prevent anyone from forcing entry, video-type doorbells are great as they give you video footage too in case you need it for evidence and you can see if anyone comes to your door even when you aren't at home.

Think about what you might do if an incident was to happen at home – play it through in advance so that you are prepared, how would you get out, what could you say, think about a code to use with a trusted family member to alert them to call for help.

Of course, the safest thing is to not allow your abuser into your home if at all possible – always arrange handovers for the children elsewhere, even if that is by the front gate, your home, should be your safe place.

 Can you organise handovers at school or somewhere there is CCTV? Somewhere the children feel safe and comfortable is always good but just make sure it is in public and consider how you will get there and back at different times of year too as in winter it gets dark early.

Be vigilant

Change your routines if you are worried about stalking. Make sure someone knows where you are going and when to expect you. If something worries you, it just doesn't feel right and you are concerned your ex is following you or harassing you, report it. Don't be worried about wasting police time or getting it wrong – much better to be safe than sorry and if it is stalking, this behaviour needs to be dealt with quickly.

Digital Stalking

Change your passwords! This is one for the first things you should do in any case – to your emails, your social media accounts, your online shopping accounts, anything your ex could possibly hack into. Check your mobile too for any spyware - take it to a mobile phone shop and ask them to check it for you. Be mindful if you are still with your abuser – work out a code with professionals, so they know it is you texting, in case your abuser gets access to your phone, you may also want to store their details under a pseudonym.

Keep evidence too – never delete any communication from your abuser. You may think it is irrelevant as non-threatening but it may show a pattern of controlling behaviour and you may want it as evidence in future. Don't change your telephone number, it is better to know how your abuser is thinking than to be completely in the dark.

Breaches

Know what to do if your ex breaches any restrictions – for an injunction or breach of Bail conditions you can report to police. If it is a breach of a Child Arrangement Order or an Order obtained through Civil Court, you will have to contact your solicitor. However, if you are fearful, if there are threats being made or you are scared at all, please call 999.

Remember if you have to call police, this is as a result of your abuser's behaviour – don't feel guilty. Protect yourself first, everything else can be sorted out afterwards.

High Risk Indicators

If you recognise any of these behaviours below then beware. These are all potentially fatal and mean that your abuser has the capacity to seriously harm you in future. Perpetrators think alike and often act alike and it means we can predict what they might do in future. Women die each year because they never think their partner is capable of such things, because they think 'he would never do that to me'. Don't ignore these warnings!

Separation – Most women murdered by their partners (ex) die within 3 months of separation. Don't think that because you are separated you are safe or because your partner has never physically hurt you, you are safe. Be vigilant – make sure you have a safety plan in place and update this as your circumstances change. Remember this relationship is based on power and control and leaving is the worst thing imaginable to an abuser – they will want to get you back or punish you for leaving.

Conflict around child contact – If they can't get to you directly, of course, the next best thing is to try and control you through the children or use them as a way to seek revenge. Get legal advice on how best to protect you and your children. Get a robust safety plan in place – include the schools and nurseries in this.

Isolation –If you are trying to do this alone it can be very tough. Get support and it is so much easier.

Pregnancy – Babies can be injured due to domestic abuse and assault. Holding your baby is not necessarily going to protect you against an assault. Pregnancy is often a time when emotional abuse and controlling behaviour increases. Don't think that having a baby will make your situation better, it won't.

Strangulation – It's a fine line between choking someone and strangling them. Strangulation is one of the most common ways women die from domestic abuse (being stabbed is the other). If this is happening to you, don't wait for things to get better. Next time it could be too late.

Threats to kill themselves or you – This is so common. They want you to feel guilty for leaving them, they want to shift your attention away from trying to recover. They want you to feel afraid – for them, for you, for your children, for your family. We always believe threats because you never know if they just might carry them out – however, remember, this is a tactic and their wellbeing is not your responsibility. This can sound harsh, but you have to put your wellbeing first.

Weapons – If someone has access to weapons or training which gives them additional skills, such as martial arts, then this needs to be incorporated into your safety plan. Don't let this stop you from leaving – just be aware of the risk and put plans in place to manage it.

Escalation of abuse – Once abuse occurs within a relationship there is no going back. It will only get worse. If you notice things are getting worse, incidents are happening more frequently or the violence is increasing, don't wait and hope that things will improve. They won't.

Staying shows the abuser that they can get away with it – it lets them feel comfortable, they don't worry about you calling police or leaving because they have done this before and nothing happened. If there are no consequences to their actions there is no reason to stop. What will it take for you to realise that enough is enough?

Stalking – This is obsessive behaviour. Your partner or ex is constantly thinking about you and thinking up of ways to find out information about you, to convince you to get back with them or to convince others that you are meant to be together. This behaviour can go on for months or even years if you don't get professional help and put measures in place to stop it.

Criminal History – If your abuser has a history of domestic abuse or violence, he is highly unlikely to change. In fact – forget that, he is never going to change. He will have moved from one relationship to the next, continuing the same patterns of behaviour, probably getting worse each time. If he has been in prison before, will he really be worried about going back there again? Will he take notice of consequences?

If he has started a domestic abuse programme through probation or voluntarily it can actually increase the risk to you. This is because the abuser has to reflect on lots of very difficult issues – they may be challenged on their thinking, encouraged to take responsibility for assaults, have to consider how their behaviour affects their children.

Opening up this 'can of worms' can make it difficult for the abuser to cope and their behaviour can get worse as they begin to address these issues. They will be taught coping strategies and supported by the group facilitators but don't expect them to go on this programme and become a completely different person by the end of it. It is very difficult to change behaviours and beliefs that have been embedded for many years. Focus on the changes that are within your control instead of pinning all your hopes on your abuser to change.

So, there are many things to be worried about when ending an abusive relationship but remember, knowledge is power.

Now you know what to look out for, you can understand how to protect yourself. Get people to help you. Be vigilant at all times. Stay strong.

CHAPTER 3:
RECOVERY

The emotional rollercoaster

When you go through any big life change it causes a whole wave of emotion. Whether it is the end of a relationship (no matter whose decision it was), the loss of a job, a bereavement, moving house, or a health scare, these experiences all cause shockwaves.

It all starts with **Shock and Denial** – you might avoid thinking about your ex, 'put your head in the sand' and hope that when you look back up everything will have gone back to normal. You may avoid dealing with your situation at all. You may struggle to think clearly at all – your head can often feel like it is stuffed with cotton wool. You may find you have short-term memory loss, that you struggle to articulate how you feel, to remember important details or even just to remember appointments.

"Thank goodness my IDVA was with me at the first solicitor's appointment! The solicitor asked me to explain what had happened and I couldn't – I just went blank. My IDVA had to

remind me to mention the details. So much had happened over the years, I had forgotten some of the abuse."

After shock, comes **Anger and frustration**. You may feel angry that you have wasted so much time in a bad relationship, you may be angry at the lies you are hearing from your ex, you may feel frustrated that you are left in debt and having to manage the 'fallout'.

"I couldn't believe it! He denied everything! He twisted it and said that I had caused it all. He told his solicitor that I was just upset because I had discovered him having an affair. He forgot to mention everything else he had done in the past few years – how he put me down all the time, calling me names in front of the kids, never letting me out of his sight and isolating me from all my friends. He forced me to take out loans to cover his gambling debts too!"

Bargaining is where you are trying to find some reasoning, some explanation for what has happened. You may also have lots of 'why' questions and 'what if' questions about the future. You may feel guilty and ashamed, especially if your children are struggling to come to terms with the separation. Remember, this wasn't what you wanted from your relationship - you didn't go into it knowing he was abusive, you never wanted it to end, but it had to. Remember the reasons why the relationship ended.

"I kept asking him why he had done it but he couldn't come up with an answer. He just said he gets angry sometimes – that he finds life difficult and that he would go to counselling. He has been going since February and I just have to think about whether I am prepared to wait much longer for things to change."

In the next wave there comes **Depression and Sadness** as you realise that you are where you are. You can't go back in time, you grieve for the losses and you may start to realise the enormity of your situation.

"I just couldn't get out of bed for days. I cried and cried like my heart would break, and for why? For a man who didn't deserve me. I realised I couldn't keep feeling like this – I spoke to my GP and got some help. I still have bad days but I know I deserve better!"

You will gradually start to feel stronger as time passes and you know you have to move on, you start making plans and thinking about the future. **Acceptance** is just that – accepting that you are here now, it is what it is. You can look back at your ex and your relationship without feeling the sharp pain of the emotion. You get a different perspective – you are stronger, more detached from it, focussing more on you rather than on him and starting to find yourself again.

You may be trying out new things, setting new goals, thinking about what you want for your future now it is different to the one you previously imagined – and you feel ok about it, you might even feel excited about it!

"I can talk about it now without getting upset. It's like I am talking about someone else's story because I feel like a different person now."

It's a process. There may be days when you feel strong and motivated and then days where you feel exhausted with little energy or will to think about the future. Accept this is normal, you are not a robot, you have feelings – don't fight against the waves. If you are having a crap day, accept it. It's your mind and body telling you it needs time and space to recover.

You may even get all the way to acceptance and then something might happen to upset you and you may slip back down to depression again. If that happens, get some good support, think about why this happened.

Is it something that you can control or not? Is there something you could do differently to get yourself up and out of the depression and to move forwards again?

Can you learn from this and put some strategies in place to make sure that this doesn't happen again?

Grief Cycle

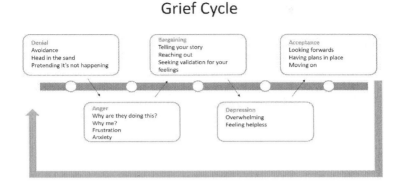

'Disney' relationship versus reality

When a relationship ends, we often look back at it through 'rose-tinted spectacles. We focus on all the good bits, minimise and excuse the bad behaviour or ignore it. We see the 'Disney' version of our relationship! Cinderella, Prince Charming, hearts, flowers and singing birds!

Was it really that bad? What if he does change? What if I try harder? An abuser is rarely bad all the time, so there will have been good times somewhere – but were these genuinely good times or part of the cycle of abuse I mentioned earlier?

Reality check time! Compare what you wanted your relationship to be like (the Disney version) versus the reality (which is likely to be quite different). Remember how it felt when you were scared of your ex, when you were 'walking on eggshells'.

Now think about how nice it is now that you don't have to do that anymore – if you are still together, think about how nice it would be to be able to do this. Imagine waking up in a peaceful home, no threats, no bullying, no criticism. Remember exactly what your worth is and don't let yourself slip back into thinking that this relationship was better than it actually was. Keep moving on, step by step and day by day it will get easier.

Fear, Anxiety and Overwhelm

When you are under threat, your primitive brain kicks in – the 'fight, flight or freeze' response is activated. This is your way of protecting yourself from potential harm and you have no control over it. You may lash out, you may run away or you may freeze, unable to speak, shout out or scream. When you are experiencing constant levels of stress, fear and anxiety, because of domestic abuse you are in a constant state of 'fight, flight or freeze'.

You may cry, shake, feel panicky, vomit, feel angry or anxious after an incident has occurred and shock sets in. If you feel yourself hyper-ventilating or spiralling into a panic attack, cup your hands over your nose and mouth and just keep breathing in and out. Your breathing will naturally slow down and you will feel much calmer within a couple of minutes. It's a really simple technique, but it works.

Grounding techniques really work for anxiety and overwhelm.

- Focus on 5 things you can see around you – can you see the trees, the clock on the wall, what else can you see?

- Move on to 4 things you feel and so on. Really focus.

- Again, this is a really simple technique using the power of the senses and this technique will quickly calm you.

- Remind yourself of where you are now. What options do you have now? What can you do to take control of this situation? Once you take back some control you will feel less anxious and less overwhelmed.

Anger and Frustration

It is normal to feel angry and frustrated from time to time – after all, you don't deserve to be abused! The trick is to turn these negative feelings into something more positive and constructive that serves you better. Instead of venting your anger at your ex, do something positive with it. Release the anger by doing some exercise – go for a run or do a workout, punch a pillow or have a good cry to release those emotions and then shake it off.

Sometimes you need to let it all out, so do so, and then physically stand up, shake your arms and your legs and then move on. Distract yourself, put on some happy music, do something to keep busy or take some action to make your situation better. Exercise is also a great mood booster and can really help you cope better during these prolonged periods of stress. Don't let your abuser control your mood – you can control it!

Depression and Suicidal Thoughts

It is absolutely normal to experience some level of depression when you are in an abusive and controlling relationship. You are not a robot – you are human, with feelings. Feelings of hopelessness can lead to despair and subsequently to suicidal thoughts.

People experiencing domestic abuse are highly likely to experience depression and suicidal thoughts and most women who are hospitalised due to mental health issues have a history of domestic abuse. If you feel like this you are not alone. Don't be afraid to reach out – speak to your GP or call a crisis helpline such as Samaritans or Sane (the numbers are in the back of this book). Don't be worried about taking medication if it will help you cope better – there are many, many people who take this nowadays for all sorts of reasons, not just domestic abuse. Getting the help that you need can be seen as a positive step.

Counselling may help, coaching definitely will, as this will give you the strategies to feel more in control of your situation. Most important of all is that you get support from someone who understands domestic abuse. Alternative therapies can help relax you, meditation is clinically proven to reduce anxiety. These activities won't change your situation but they will help you cope better and it is really important for you to factor time each week to do this. Taking time just for you is vital for your recovery.

If the panic attacks and post-traumatic stress symptoms are too difficult to manage by yourself there are some great therapists that can help you. Rapid eye movement therapy (EMDR) has had some great reviews in recent years – it is a particular type of psychotherapy and works by using the client's eye movements to dampen down the power of traumatic events. Remember, you can't erase what has already happened to you, but you can learn techniques and use strategies to stop it affecting you as much.

If you feel suicidal please reach out to specialist services – you can call them or txt them for free and many of them operate out of hours. Remember these feelings will pass. They happen because of the abuse you have experienced, which is not your fault. They are difficult emotions, but they will pass and with help you can feel better. You CAN get through it – you CAN move on and be happy again, you CAN get support to help you.

Learn to recognise what makes you feel better. Even if you don't feel like doing these things, push yourself to. Recognise the difference it makes – even if it is a small change, it is change. Take responsibility for your own happiness. Take control back and create the life you deserve.

The Stages of Change

This is the process each person goes through when trying to end an abusive relationship. You may go through each stage quickly, move forwards and then slip backwards again. Some people move through stages slowly because they don't feel strong enough or perhaps don't have much support or because practical issues prevent them moving forwards. Everyone's journey through this cycle is different. Don't get frustrated, understand where you are in this cycle and keep striving forwards.

Pre-contemplation (Denial)

This is when you are in denial – it's just too difficult to hear, too much to accept, to know that your partner – the one who is supposed to love and care for you is actually intent on abusing you and controlling you, is overwhelming. It is easier to ignore it, hope it will get better, try harder.

Contemplation (Thinking about it)

Someone has 'planted the seed' – they may have challenged your thinking '' do you think the way he spoke to you was ok?'' '' I don't like the way he gets so jealous'', '' you have changed, you don't seem yourself''. They have shown concern about your relationship and how it is affecting you. You may have seen something about domestic abuse on TV, that made you think 'that's me'.

Action

Doing something about it – this might not necessarily mean leaving. It may be doing some research on your options should you choose to leave or reaching out to talk about it to someone for the first time. At this point you know that something has to change and you are starting to take responsibility for your own happiness – prioritising you.

Maintenance

This can be the tricky part – sometimes the leaving is easy but staying away is hard. Loneliness, maybe having to move to a smaller home, struggling to cope with the children alone, financial worries, can all lead you to think that going back might be an easier option. This is the time when you need to have a good support team around you and when you must keep using those strategies to keep you strong.

Relapse

You may return home to the abuser or start to communicate with them again. You may listen to their apologies, their promises to change and believe them. If you do find yourself back with your abuser, don't lose hope. Many women leave and go back – often several times before they leave for good. Try again.

Coping Strategies – the early days

Knowing how to cope in the early days after separation is vital. It will feel weird, lonely and un-nerving, this is not what you are used to. It is only a short period of time though – you will have lots of great times ahead of you, you just need to get through this tricky bit first. Using these strategies will really help you stay strong.

Tell people

Tell people you have left. If you tell people it's a fact, right? Try not to make excuses or say you are 'having a break'. Don't excuse your abuser's behaviour – say it as it is, you have nothing to be ashamed of. You don't have to go into details, in fact you will probably find that some people will have already guessed what happened. Don't go over and over it either, re-telling your story to everyone. You need to be focussed on the future now and focussed on getting stronger.

Cut the cord

They will try every trick in the book to get you back – don't believe any of it! If you still have to have some communication with them, do it through your solicitor or makes sure you set the boundaries around your communication with them. Nip it in the bud – don't get involved in long conversations with your ex, keep it short. Don't respond to all their messages and keep very clear boundaries with them. They need to know you aren't coming back.

Once you have recognised that your relationship is unhealthy you need to cut the cord – detach yourself from them, take all of the emotion out of it. You need to cut the emotional attachment to the person who is abusive – 'cutting the cord' is a technique that will protect you from emotional harm in future and potentially physical harm too. When you metaphorically cut the cord, you see the abuser through different eyes –no matter what they say, it won't affect you.

When I tried to leave, my ex used to talk 'at' me until the early hours of the morning, telling me all the reasons why I shouldn't leave until I was so exhausted, I would give in. Of course, nothing changed. It was only when I finally 'cut the cord', that I suddenly felt strong enough to leave and stay away. It didn't matter how much he begged or pleaded it meant nothing. I didn't feel sorry for him, I didn't feel angry, I felt nothing. I saw him for what he was – someone who was insecure, jealous and controlling. I knew I deserved better and so do you.

Boundaries

With 'cutting the cord' comes boundaries. You must keep those boundaries up, keep communication brief and to the point, don't get caught off guard.

A simple text message from them can soon turn into 'text tennis' back and forth all day long. They send you a text first thing in the morning or last thing at night knowing full well this will set the tone for your day or keep you up all night worrying. Remember they want you to be thinking about them no matter what. Keep it simple and brief, keep those strong boundaries in place. Don't let those text messages interfere with your day – answer it or don't answer it, you decide, then get on with your day or get some sleep.

You may put your phone on silent at night so any texts can be dealt with in the morning or better still get yourself a cheap mobile phone just to communicate with your ex so you can put it away in a drawer when you don't want to look at it. See the text message, consider what they are really asking or what do they really want and decide how you want to deal with it. There is always some underlying motive. Remember these are only words – you can't control what they say but how much or how little they affect you is up to you.

If your ex is continuously breaching contact arrangements then consider taking this back to Court and amending your Child Arrangement Order or reasserting your boundaries with your ex. Work out what you can do to take control over this – instead of waiting around because he never tells you what time he will be there to collect the children, offer to drop them off to his. Think of strategies that work for you.

Keep evidence

If you are getting long, ranting txt messages – this may be classed as harassment. If you find it upsetting to read their messages, learn how to speed read – for example, read the bits that are important and miss out the other bits which are just designed to stress you. Some people use friends or relatives to help filter the communication – they read it for you and then summarise any bits that you really need to know. They aren't emotionally attached to the abuser, so it can often be less traumatic for them to read these messages and it protects you from a barrage of emotional abuse.

"my ex used to send me long emails, but only about 1/3 used to be stuff related to what we had to discuss. The rest was pure venom, just him criticising my parenting and spouting pure anger. I learnt quickly to filter these, so I didn't read them in detail and just picked out the bits that mattered. For others, I just ignored them completely."

Keep your guard up

Don't take calls or messages from your ex for the first few days at least. They will try everything to get you back - crying, pleading, promising to change, threats. Don't change your number - it can be helpful to know what kind of mood they are in especially if they are making threats and particularly if they have begun stalking.

Don't respond to the contacts, don't listen to the calls and messages or the lies– remember they know exactly how to get to you, to make you feel guilty. Keep texts and emails as evidence – you may not want to report your ex to police right now, but always keep things like this just in case you need to report him in future. If you feel threatened, I strongly encourage you to report this to police – even if nothing comes of it, it is a log of events, evidence of a pattern of behaviour and it validates your concerns.

Brave the Wave.

This bit can be tough, but use the technique called 'Brave the Wave'. If you do hear or read anything from your ex - detach the emotion from it, remember you are not responsible for them, you don't have to listen to their voice any more, or hear their excuses. You are focussing on you, nobody else, so let what your ex's words wash right over your head like a huge wave - remember the things they say are all tactics - pre-meditated, designed to tug at your heartstrings.

Your ex knows exactly how to get to you, so don't let them. Stay calm, focus on the things around you, the people around you, the other noises around you and their voice will become quieter and less powerful. Just let that wave of words wash over you, breathe deeply, stay calm, stay focussed. Visualise the words washing over your head and down your back, creating a puddle of water on the floor that will soon disappear and dry up in the sun. Once dried, the words are gone forever.

They will use any means to try and get to you. If your abuser knows you suffer from a lack of confidence about your parenting, what is the first thing they will have a go at? Yes, exactly that – they will begin accusing you of being an unfit parent.

 If they know you don't have the support of friends/family (probably because they have already isolated you from them) they will tell you nobody will believe you if you leave, that you can't cope on your own without them, that they will never leave you alone - little jibes and comments designed to get inside your head and niggle away at you - all part of their strategy to keep control over you at all costs. Remember, just because they say it, it doesn't mean it is true and it doesn't mean people will believe it.

Practice this 'Brave the Wave' technique – give it a go!

Think before you act

Always think: Do I have to respond to this? Do I have to respond right now? How shall I respond?

This takes practice, you might be used to 'jumping' as soon as your ex demands it, but remember you are no longer with them – you don't have to justify your actions and you definitely don't have to jump when they say jump. If you have to communicate with your ex keep it brief, to the point and don't get distracted or led into conversations – it will only end up with you feeling more stressed or upset.

You can't reason with someone who is unreasonable. They will not hear the answers they want to hear - they will try everything to persuade you to agree with them, but of course you won't. This leads to frustration on their part, then anger and before you know it hours have passed and you are still having the same conversation. If you get caught out, and find yourself going round in circles, stuck in a conversation loop, end the conversation – make an excuse to end it if you have to, just stop it. Next time resolve to end the conversation quicker. If they start being abusive towards you, cut the conversation dead and refuse to engage.

Take back the control – you don't deserve to be shouted at, abused or put down and if they can't stop themselves then you can choose not to speak with them!

"I started responding to his emails at the end of each week as there would be a daily barrage of emails, all pages long. It was too stressful! I started to deal with them at the end of each week after scanning through the main points and then I would summarise everything in one email, keeping it light and positive, whereas he expects me to be angry. This works so much better – it probably winds him up because I don't immediately respond and ignore lots of his points, but it makes it much easier for me to cope with."

Surround yourself with positive people.

Try not to talk constantly about your ex - have a bit of respite if you can to just 'be'. Reach out to family or friends who can help build you up again – positive people who can help you feel more confident and positive about yourself again. It's ok to laugh, to talk about their lives rather than yours, to talk about nothing at all, just 'be' around people again. Get used to being in a peaceful environment, enjoy doing the things that make you happy and just get some 'headspace'. Positive people will be encouraging, their positive vibes will help you through.

Create your own support team to help you - professionals, friends, colleagues or family. Whoever it is, they need to be non-judgemental, supportive, able to challenge your thinking if you are having a 'wobbly day' and able to keep you motivated. Having this team will help you feel stronger – please reach out to them as and when you need to, don't struggle on alone because you don't want to bother anyone.

Bin the past.

It can really help to stop taking your contraceptive Pill, throw away the sexy underwear you hated wearing just to please him, you may even want to take off your wedding ring. Change the furniture around – get some new bedding, put the pillows in the middle of the bed so you can't see an obvious space where your ex used to sleep, put the wedding photos away.

Doing these little things might seem quite trivial and un-important in the grand scheme of things but what they do is remind you that this time is the last time and remind you that you have left for good. Physically changing your environment helps stop the triggers and reminders of the past. Move the photos of your ex into the children's bedrooms, so you don't have to see them all the time or put them away in a box. Remember, you don't have to try and forget the happy times, but you can reframe your memories – focussing on the good bits and choosing not to remember the bad bits. Embrace the sense of freedom you have now, put up the pictures you were never allowed to, make your own rules.

'' I donated my wedding dress to a charity that organises funerals for terminally ill couples. It was comforting to know that someone else could create some cherished memories with the dress and it helped me move on because I didn't want to look at it anymore.''

Choose what to believe.

If you hear someone trying to defend your ex remember they only know one side of the story. Don't waste your energy trying to convince them of the truth – you know the truth and that is all that matters. When your friend tells you that they have seen your ex and he is sooo sorry and looks awful – remember this is a tactic designed to gain sympathy from you and other people who might be of use to him.

He will tell friends he has no food in the fridge and can't cope without you but if you actually looked in the fridge it would be full and all he is missing is you cooking it for him! You may have to ask them not to tell you all the latest updates on his activities as it can become quite emotionally draining. Ask them to tell you if there is anything significant you need to know about, but otherwise, keep it quiet.

Pause before making decisions.

Deal with the immediate issues – how to keep yourself safe first and foremost and where you are going to stay in the short-term. Get specialist advice before you make big decisions on issues like finances and housing and don't make big decisions based purely on emotion, as these decisions can affect your life for a long time to come – some of the decisions you have to make can be delayed for a while until you are a bit stronger and can think more clearly. You will feel very differently in 6 months' time to how you feel in the immediate aftermath of leaving.

Think about:

Do I need to decide on this right now? Can it wait? Do I need to find out more information first?

Who can I speak to do get some more clarity on this? A Divorce Coach? A solicitor? A financial advisor? Your mum? Your sensible best friend? A website?

At first you may be adamant that you want to remain in the marital home, but further down the line you may change your mind and feel desperate to move on and start afresh. Don't make hasty decisions you might regret. It can be tough thinking about moving out of the home you have lived in for many years, but if it is crumbling around you or your children are likely to move out of home in the next few years, is it really worth keeping it at all costs?

Moving into a smaller, more secure property that requires little maintenance and has no connection to your ex can be the kick-start to your new life. You can make this move exciting - instead of thinking about what you have lost, think about what you have gained — cheaper bills, less maintenance, the chance to make it truly yours.

"At first, I was adamant I didn't want to leave our home, but once I was near the end of the proceedings I couldn't wait to move out. My new property has absolutely nothing to do with him — I decorated it in colours I liked but he hated and made it cosy, whereas he always had to have it minimalistic. I love it!"

Protect your finances.

Not only in the immediate period after leaving, but to secure your future. Economic abuse is extremely common — being forced to take out loans in your name, being persuaded to sign documents that you have little understanding of related to finances, not being allowed access to your own money are just some examples of economic abuse.

"My ex was always insistent on us having a joint bank account – when I left him, he cleared it out and left me with £10 for myself and my child. When we got the mortgage agreed, he had insisted on it being a joint mortgage. I put the whole deposit down but wasn't aware I could have protected that and when we divorced, he was in control of the house sale - he sold the house and I was left with nothing."

- Check if you can secure your property with the Land Registry. This will prevent your ex selling the house from underneath you or being mortgaged without your consent. If you are registered on the mortgage or as having an interest in a property, doing this will make sure that your ex can't sell the property without your consent and you can sign up for alerts to notify you if attempts are made. Your ex will be notified by them though, so think about how they might react and how you might manage this before you go ahead.

- Talk to your bank. If you have a joint account you won't be allowed to close it without your ex's consent but make them aware that you have separated and talk to them about any options to protect your money from being withdrawn by your ex.

- Talk to creditors – if you are likely to be struggling financially after your separation, let them know your situation. Don't ignore payments, most creditors will offer you reduced payments or interest-only payments for a period of time to make things a bit easier. Go to the "Sources of Help" section at the back of this book to see who can help you with this.

- Remember if you are fleeing to an area unknown to your abuser, don't use cashpoints until you have changed your account details and make sure you don't get bank statements sent to your previous home address in the interim!

- Make sure you get all the Benefits and income you are entitled to. Transferring Child Benefit can take many weeks to change so get cracking with it. You will be entitled to 'single persons' Council Tax rebate, as well as other allowances, so always check if there are any single person discounts when setting up new utilities and accounts.

You may have less income initially but at least it will be yours. Yours to manage, without having to justify any spending. Financial independence is important – being able to manage your own money will stop you from feeling vulnerable in future. The quicker you can become financially independent from your ex, the better.

Recharge.

If you struggle to sleep, rest when you can. You need your energy to recover and to keep your mind clear for those times when you need to be strong or to make important decisions. Have a wind-down routine before bed – this is often the time when your mind starts racing, use the last bit of the evening for some 'me' time, remind yourself of the things you have to be grateful for before bed.

"I slept the best I had in years when I left and my appetite came back. The neck pain I thought was a long-term complaint miraculously cleared up, it just shows you the stress and tension I was under at home."

Puncture your stress bucket.

Focus on doing things that help you feel better at the same time as dealing with all the practical stuff, the stuff that tends to cause you stress. Imagine a bucket filling up more and more to the brim with stress and then imagine puncturing a hole in it at the bottom. The hole allows the stress to seep out slowly so the bucket never overflows. The things that help calm you, that relieve your stress levels, that help you cope better are the metaphorical hole in your bucket.

You need to cope well in order to think clearly and make good decisions. Things like mindfulness, meditation, yoga, Pranic healing, are all brilliantly simple practices that help distract you from overthinking, prevent overwhelm by bringing your thoughts back to the present and encourage you to de-stress. If you have never tried them before, give them a go. Whilst these techniques won't solve your situation, they will help you cope better and give your head some space just to be calm and they will help quieten your mind.

"I make sure I do some exercise in the morning or meditation at night, because I know I feel stronger when I do it. It helps me feel good about myself and helps me switch off from everything else."

Stuffing your emotions.

Try not to keep so busy that you actually end up exhausting yourself and burning out. You are trying hard not to feel the hurt, the anxiety the stress, the overwhelm so you block them out- partying too hard, drinking too much, working long hours, using drugs or having casual sex to 'prove' you are moving on. All of these strategies are counter-productive and leave you feeling pretty rubbish after a while. Don't stuff them away – face your fears and deal with them.

Feed your soul.

You need your energy and some clarity to be able to think clearly. Drink plenty water – our brains don't function properly if we are dehydrated. Try not to drink too much alcohol as this is a depressant too. Eat well, eat healthily, feel good about yourself, take time to nourish you – you deserve it. Choose the foods you like to eat. If you feel a bit nauseous with stress or anxiety or have lost your appetite, eat little and often – don't worry, your appetite will come back. Healthy body, healthy mind!

" You can't pour from an empty cup"

Be You again.

When you have been told what to wear, what music to listen to, who you can talk to, you lose your sense of self. Start to find YOU again – take some time to find out what you like doing, who you like talking to, open up your mind to new possibilities.

Was there something you had to give up because of your relationship – could you re-start it? Would you like to use your experience to do something different?

Going through divorce or separation can put lots of things in perspective – maybe you want to do a job that is more meaningful now or maybe now you have the opportunity to go for a promotion that would have been impossible previously? This is your chance to re-design your life. Don't just do the same old things just because. You have choice and control over your life now and you can be anything you want to be!

Write it down.

If you have recently ended an abusive relationship there are so many things to consider that it can be a struggle to think clearly. It's like your brain is trying to protect you by filtering out the amount of information it can cope with. Write things down – take a notepad and pen to every meeting, every appointment. Carry it around with you so you can jot down notes as and when you think of them – thoughts and ideas will come to you at random times, when you least expect it.

You will have a million and one things going around your head. Write down how you feel, if you feel angry or upset writing it down can be very cathartic and better to write it down than spill it all out in a venomous text or email to your ex that can then be used against you further down the line. If you are tempted to reach out to your ex write down what you want to say but don't send it – go away, do something else, then come back to it and read it again.

Do you really want to send it? What do you think their reaction might be? Is there something else you can do to make yourself feel better? Could you reach out to a friend or family member instead?

If you need to communicate with your ex or a professional but are worried you aren't quite getting it right, have someone else look at it first. It's easy to fill your email with emotion but is that helping you get your point across or is it diluting the important stuff you need to say? Can you condense it down, keep it factual?

Wobbly Days.

Of course, you will have these! One day you will wake up feeling strong and fierce and other days you will feel low, tearful and exhausted. Think about what it is that you can do in this moment to make yourself feel better or to make your situation better. Put up post-it notes to remind you of how to do this – write the words 'Do' on one and 'Feel' on the other.

Can you 'do' something – write an email to your solicitor, pick up the phone to one of your support team, find out some information to give you some clarity?

Can you 'feel' better by going for a walk or a run, putting on some uplifting music, reminding yourself of why you left, taking some time to enjoy something you can do now that you couldn't do before?

The wobbly days will become less frequent the stronger you become. Don't think too far ahead – just go from moment to moment. Get through one hour, then one day, one week and so on and it will get easier.

Don't show your emotions.

Showing emotional upset to a narcissist is like adding fuel to a fire. Narcissists thrive on drama – seeing you upset or angry makes them feel like they have won – so the best thing you can do it is not show them any reaction. No matter how difficult it is, how much you want to cry or scream or shout, don't. Leave it till you get home – rise above any nasty comments, remember your abuser knows exactly how to get to you, the things to say that hurt you the most and the lies to make you angry - they will try and provoke you at any opportunity and when you least expect it.

Be prepared for this – practice how you will react. Take a deep breath, stay calm, you can even catch them off guard and be ultra- polite to them when you know they are ready for an argument! Whatever they do or say, act as if it doesn't bother you at all. You may hear this technique referred to as 'grey rock'. Essentially you want to seem as boring as any old grey rock on a beach. When you have to engage with your ex talk about boring things, nothing that can cause any drama. Don't try to get them to see how unreasonable they are being or let them know how their behaviour affects you.

Hold your head high, shoulders back and breathe slowly – remember you are in control now. Offering no reaction gives your abuser nothing to react back to and completely dissolves the situation. It pours water on their fire! Of all the coping strategies this technique is probably the most powerful of all.

'' My ex used to sit and say all these things, trying to make himself look clever, trying to provoke an argument or make me angry. I used to sit there and smile, be polite, ignore it, thinking what an absolute moron he was, using his time and energy trying to trigger a fight. I would walk away, I would get on with my day, and I just knew he would be left feeling frustrated that he didn't get the fight he wanted. Once I figured out that this technique worked, it made coping with him that much easier and eventually he stopped trying to wind me up because he knew it just didn't work on me anymore.''

Avoid your ex

Avoid the places where your ex is likely to be. You don't want to go to the same shops, pub or places where you used to go with him. Go to different shops, different pubs or different places, reduce the risk of bumping into him for now and start creating new happier memories. You might not always be able to avoid him, but it will make things easier in the immediate period after leaving. If you have to see him, see him in a public place – somewhere safer, where there are other people around, where you can leave if you want to and where they are less likely to be confrontational.

Don't stalk your ex on social media either and ask friends not to report back to you unless it is something really important that you need to know.

''My friend told me my ex was telling everyone on Facebook he had Schizophrenic Personality Disorder and he had been to hospital to get help. Police told me there was no record of any hospital admission and when he had been assessed by a clinician, they had found no history or symptoms related to this disorder at all. He was saying it all so people would feel

sorry for him and so they wouldn't realise the truth – that he had intentionally hurt me and his own children."

Mutual friends can be tricky, you may cope better if you don't see some of these friends for a while – let them know this might not be forever, but just because of the situation right now and if they are true friends they will understand. Don't make life more difficult for yourself. You need to try and make a new life for yourself, with no reminders of the past.

If you simply can't avoid your ex, practice scenarios and how you might deal with this situation. If you bump into him at the pub will you leave or be able to ignore him or can you choose to go to a different pub for a while.

You might be thinking 'why should I have to go somewhere different when I haven't done anything wrong?' but this is about making your life easier in the short-term, not about who is right and wrong. You can choose to make your life easier – who needs the drama?! Go to a different pub and relax, rather than looking over your shoulder.

Change your name.

You may not want to do this straight away -or you might! Changing your surname back to your maiden name needs no court document. You are allowed to refer back to your maiden name any time you want, except for changing your passport and your driving licence. For those, you will need a Decree Absolute. Reclaim your identity – be 'YOU' again.

It can be quite liberating and again gives yourself and everyone else a signal that you are moving on. Bear in mind that you will not be able to change your children's surnames without your ex's permission or until they come of age and can change it themselves by Deed Poll. Think about how the children will feel – are they happy for you to change it back?

Small steps, big changes.

You may think to yourself that some of the strategies above are so small that they won't make any difference, but what they do is build up to bigger changes overall. One change at a time helps you move forwards and by breaking things down into small, manageable strategies, you will feel more in control, less overwhelmed and will start to see quick progress. This is important in the early stages when everything feels weird and when you feel so vulnerable. Refer to the points above, put them into action and see how they help.

The key to feeling good is to decide to stop feeling bad

It's your life, so live it!

Remember this difficult time with court proceedings, divorce or the early stages of separation is just a short time in the grand scheme of things. Stay strong and you will get through it - imagine how great your life can be going forwards! It probably feels like the toughest time, that it is never-ending, but remember where you have been and where you are going – you WILL get there and the rest of your life can be amazing!

Freedom is what you are fighting for, so don't give up. Remember what you have already been through – you are stronger than you think. Be a role model – show your children, your friends, your family and yourself how strong you are and live the life you deserve!

You have your support tribe – you might have re-established relationships with friends and family already and now you can start to create new happier memories. It sounds so easy, doesn't it?! I don't mean to be flippant – of course it isn't easy, but if you use these strategies, it CAN happen!

Boundaries

Keep them up! This is a must! Don't let them slip for a second! Be tough and be consistent – do what is right for you and the children. Don't feel guilty about saying 'no' if it doesn't work for you. As a caring, empathetic person you care. Sometimes caring so much leaves us wide open to being taken advantage of. An abuser knows that and will try any way to manipulate these boundaries – they hate being told what they can and can't do! Start to put your needs first. This is your life and now is your chance to make it the best. If you let those boundaries slip, before you know it your ex will have found a way to take back some of the control. You need to be in control.

Gratitude List

When you come out of an abusive relationship, you really appreciate the simple things – being able to make your own choices, not feeling afraid every time your mobile flashes, not having to justify your actions, feeling free. The little things other people take for granted can mean so much – having a bubble bath and nurturing YOU without having a time limit, relaxing on the sofa with a good book, without panicking he might walk in from work in a foul mood, having a full night's sleep, without being woken up for sex, the list goes on.

Try not to dwell on the past, you can't change it – remember why it ended and move on. Think about everything and everyone you are grateful for. You may remember incidents where people did things to help you, you may be grateful for situations – having your children with you, leaving when you did, having your 'lightbulb moment'. Small things, big things – write them, draw them, stick pictures on to represent things you are grateful for – however you want to do it, make it visual and stick it up somewhere you can easily see it.

You have many things to be grateful for – make your own Gratitude List. Stick it up on the kitchen cupboard or put it in your bedside drawer and look at it when you are having a 'wobbly' day to remind you of everything you have to be grateful for. This visual representation of gratitude will help you look forwards – shifting your focus to thinking about what you have gained rather than what you believe you have lost.

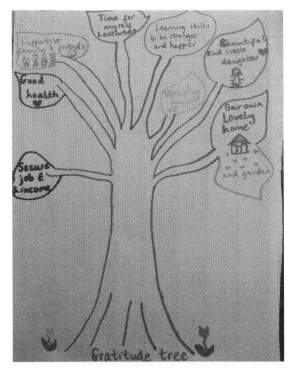

Goal setting

In the early days after a break-up, you can feel like you have lost more than you have gained. There will be plenty of 'down' days, but these will get less and less – the fogginess you feel will fade and the difficulties with short-term memory will improve. With each day you will grow in confidence – and if you have a setback, so what? It's exactly that – a setback, not the end. Shake it off, pull your metaphorical socks up and start again. Keep going – think about the short-term goals you need to achieve.

Prioritise them – tick things off your list, that's always very satisfying to do. If you only manage to achieve one thing each day, at least that is one step forward. As things start to settle down you can begin to think longer-term. Think about what you want to achieve for you going forwards – is this your chance to achieve things you were never previously allowed to? Set some bigger goals. Set 3 big goals and make them visual – take photographs, make a mood board, stick them up so you can see them often. These will keep you focussed.

Could you try and get that promotion you want? Can you start a new hobby to help you feel stronger/fitter/widen your social circle? Could you plan a holiday for you and your children – a time to bond with your children again after all the stress, a 'recovery' holiday perhaps?

"After everything we had been through with the divorce, we took a once in a lifetime trip to Australia. We explored all the sights, spent some real, quality time together and it was absolutely magical. We created great new memories, it renewed our energy and helped us mark the start of a new chapter for our family."

Imagine stepping stones to achieving those goals. For example, if the big goal is to get the promotion you want, what do you need to do to get there?

*sign up for some training to build up your skillset?

*change departments to get more practical experience?

*change your hours to suit the new role?

Make your goals realistic but think big – dream it, believe it, achieve it! If there seem to be obstacles in your way what can you do to clear them? Create your 'bucket list' – create a mood board of pictures of places you want to visit, what your future home might look like. Now is your time to re-design your life!

"I have always wanted to live by the sea, open up an animal sanctuary and write for a living. I don't want to move yet, but I can definitely start making plans and taking steps towards those bigger goals. One day I will send you a postcard with a photo of me in my new house, surrounded by animals and with my book in my hand!"

Don't let it define you

Focus on all the amazing things you can do now and the experiences you can have – try anything and everything! When you have been in an abusive relationship you have been stifled – never permitted to enjoy life, to laugh freely, to dream...but now you can! What's the worst that can happen?! Trying new things can be daunting but it can also be fun too and you will gradually start to expand your support network.

When I started to recover from my relationship breakup, I always said to myself I would never turn any invite down – when friends asked me to go out, I would say yes, every time. Even if I really didn't feel like it, I always said yes. If I had the opportunity to go somewhere, I would go. Bit by bit my confidence grew and I started to feel more independent. I COULD manage alone. I COULD make a good life for myself. I COULD. I was told for years I couldn't do so many things, but I began to realise, I could. Life is to be lived, you only get one shot, so do it - no regrets!

Negative Talk

Try not to talk about your ex in a negative way. You may need to remind relatives and friends of this too, especially if they are doing this in front of the children. Don't take up energy and time talking about someone who doesn't deserve your energy – focus on the good and positive things in your life now instead!

Don't keep repeating your story in the early days too – it can be tempting to tell everyone and to talk about it all the time as you try to understand it and make sense of it, but what this also does is keep you stuck in the 'victim' mindset. You are a survivor! Flip it round and be proud of how strong you are and how you are moving forwards – it's much nicer to talk about that instead!

It's all about balance

Remember your ex is only one part of your life, not all of your life. When you go through a separation from a controlling partner it can become all-consuming. It is the first thing you think about in the morning and the last thing you think about at night. A relationship should fit into your life, not the other way around. You need other interests, other passions and other people in your life to keep it balanced.

How you are doing in other areas of your life?

Are you spending enough time connecting with positive people, friends and family?

Are you happy in your job/career – do you want to do a course, learn new skills, go for a promotion, have a career change?

Are you feeling healthy – do you want to do more exercise, lose weight, stop smoking, reduce your stress levels?

Are you doing ok financially – can you reduce your debt, increase your income?

Are you happy with your home environment – can you change the space to make it calmer, do you want to move to a smaller home in a different area?

Fun and Leisure – are you having enough of this? Can you make more 'me' time?

Balance makes you feel happy and fulfilled, more confident and more in control. Set yourself goals and work out the baby steps you need to do to achieve them. Focus on the type of future you want and work out how you are going to achieve it – after all you are now in the driving seat.

Share your story

Domestic abuse thrives on secrecy and fear. It is powerful and scary because it has nobody to challenge it. Once you have educated yourself on how to recognise tactics of abuse, these tactics aren't nearly so scary. You know how to recognise them and so therefore you know how to deal with them. You know which ones are dangerous and how to keep yourself safe. You know which ones are just bravado and bullying.

If you can share your story with others, you will empower and inspire other victims to seek help. Women who don't yet have your confidence can see there is light at the end of the tunnel – they can see confident women like you who have come through terrible experiences but are now thriving and achieving and most importantly are HAPPY. There may be a few tears when you first start talking about it but it can be cathartic and empowering too.

Sharing your story encourages others to speak out, to tell someone, to get the help they need but are scared to ask for. You might want to write a book about it, do a magazine interview, follow through with giving evidence against your abuser or simply talk about it with women in confidential groups, do whatever feels comfortable for you.

By sharing your story, the abuser is no longer powerful. The more people that know about your story the safer you are. What was the turning point? What helped you? How do you enjoy life now compared to before? By sharing your story, you will realise just how far you have already come!

Get rid of those limiting beliefs

We all hold 'limiting beliefs' — especially if you have been in an abusive and controlling relationship. If someone tells you a hundred times that you are 'no good at this', 'incapable of that', of course, you will start to believe that. It doesn't mean it is true. You may have been brainwashed into believing that but once you are free, you can start to work out exactly what you ARE capable of. The sky is the limit!

Think of what your negative beliefs might be. Can you imagine what it might be like not to carry the weight of those negative emotions and those beliefs around with you anymore? How good will that be?!

"My ex convinced me that I could never stand up to people because he knew I had been bullied at school. The reality is that I couldn't stand up to him, because he bullied me too. Since we separated, I HAVE stood up to him, I have become more assertive and am doing things I never thought I was capable of. Now I know that I only felt like that because of him."

Can you turn these beliefs around? Find examples that contradict these beliefs — do you have evidence that might contradict those beliefs? Use more empowering words and create a new belief! I' can', I 'will'. Write a list of all the things you have achieved in a single day — this will show you just how capable you are!

Rebuilding your confidence

You have nothing to feel ashamed of. Ditch the guilt. Feel the freedom and embrace all that is good in your new life for it is far better, more colourful and more fulfilling than you ever imagined. You didn't choose for your life to go this way but it is what it is – and actually it's pretty goddamn amazing! Surround yourself with people who make you feel good about yourself, people who have similar interests to you, put yourself out there.

Your confidence will naturally be knocked because of your experience, but it can be rebuilt! Trust your abilities – just because you were always told you couldn't do things, doesn't make it true. What's the worst that could happen if you try something and it doesn't work out? It's all learning and next time it might just work. Don't worry about it. If you need to do something and you don't know how, find someone who does – or Google it or you Tube it! You are capable of many things and each time you do something successfully it will be a little tick on the list of all the things you CAN do!

You are amazing, courageous and fabulous!

Now repeat after me:

I am amazing

I am courageous

I am fabulous

I am kind

I am beautiful

I am loved

I am clever

I am ENOUGH.

Positive Thoughts, Positive Mindset

Saying a positive mantra every day can really help – you can download Apps that send you a bit of daily motivation, these help you start each day the right way. However, you have been though a lot and it is ok if you still have some 'off' days. The trick is not to fight these days, accept them, be kind to yourself, cuddle up with a soft, snuggly throw, hug your children, reach out to a friend, have an early night – whatever gets you through, then vow to start the next day in a more positive mindset. I have positive quotes everywhere in my house! On the fridge, in my living room, on the wall – these are simple things that remind you of what you have achieved so far and how strong you are.

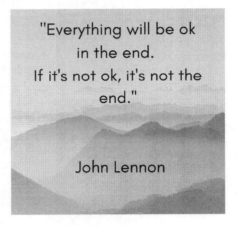

"Everything will be ok in the end. If it's not ok, it's not the end."

John Lennon

Over time, these 'off' days will become less frequent, the things that trigger you will become manageable. You can't erase the past or change it as it has already happened, but what you CAN do is change your future!

Sleep

Sleep is always one of the things that suffers when you go through periods of stress. Don't fight against it otherwise you get caught up in the cycle of: can't sleep – stressed about not being able to sleep – stress stops sleep – feel like you will never sleep again. Accept there will be days when you feel exhausted and want to sleep for England and others where you are a fully-fledged member of the 'wide awake club'. Here are some tips that might help:

- Nap when you can during the day instead

- Do some exercise earlier in the day so you feel more tired later on

- Do some relaxing exercise such as yoga in the evening

- Have a bedtime routine – bubble bath, bed, reading, no social media or TV

- Use a lavender-scented pillow spray

- Make sure your bed is cosy and warm

- Focus on how nice it is to go to sleep without criticism, demands or shouting from your ex

- Try doing a body-scan – start at your little toe, then move onto the next toe and the next, over to the other foot and so on, working your way up slowly towards your torso. Focus on the sensations – does your toe feel hot/cold, can you feel the sheet under it, is there any achiness in the toe, can you wiggle it.

This is a mindfulness technique and usually by the time you are up to your middle you are asleep! If your mind drifts back to thinking about stressful situations, don't fight it, just bring it back again and carry on with the body-scan.

This is a really great technique to practice – not only does it help you with sleeping and relieving stress but it also works as great practice for brain-training, helping you focus and compartmentalise your thoughts, so they don't become overwhelming.

You simply can't think about your situation 24 hours a day, 7 days a week, it's exhausting! Focus when you have to and at other times, bring your mind back to the present.

- Listen to one of the social Apps such as 'Calm' – relaxing music, stories, meditation to help you relax, feel less anxious and sleep.

Triggers

The mind is powerful – it can be really difficult to forget some of the things said to you, you might remember certain smells or noises that were hurtful and associated with bad experiences. If you are suffering badly with these, this is often called PTSD (Post Traumatic Stress Disorder) – there are great therapists who can help with this through a range of treatments to help reset your mind and stop these triggers from overwhelming. They can give you simple techniques and strategies that really work so don't be afraid to reach out for help if you need it.

''Every time I heard a motorbike, I thought it was my ex, even though I knew he had no idea where I lived.''

Try NOT to let these triggers overwhelm you – remember you are safe now - these triggers are only feelings and these feelings will pass. Use grounding techniques to help you. Here is a simple one:

Imagine your happy place, is it a beach? A garden? Your parent's home?

What can you smell?

What can you see?

What can you hear?

What can you taste?

What does it feel like?

If your mind starts flitting back to the trigger, don't panic, just bring it back to the happy place. Breathe deeply in through your nose, out through your mouth. Breathe in for 5 seconds, hold it for 7 seconds and breathe out for 8 seconds if you can –then shake it off.

Stand up, shake your arms, your head (gently), roll your shoulders, shake your feet then go and do something else – have a shower, make a cup of tea, go for a walk or a run, put some inspirational music on, do something to reset yourself. Remind yourself that you are safe now, these are just emotions and a natural response as your mind and body try to protect you.

Warning Signs of abuse

Knowing the warning signs to look out for is a hugely important step in your recovery. Being able to recognise these warning signs will help you feel confident enough to remove yourself from a potentially abusive relationship before it's too late.

Don't allow yourself to be pulled off centre just to have a relationship – be you, if your new partner is right for you, they will love you as you are. You matter too and you have wasted enough time putting someone else's needs way, above your own – this is your time! They either accept you and love you as you are or not at all.

Knowing the warning signs will give you the confidence to date again – why spend the rest of your life avoiding dating, avoiding a relationship that could bring you laughter and joy again? If it doesn't work out you will be ok because you know you already have a life you are happy with. If it does work out then it's a bonus!

You may spot these early on in the relationship – ignore them at your peril! Just like some of the tactics that abusers use later on, they can be subtle. Think about how their actions make you feel. Do you feel worried about challenging your partner? Do they always have to be right? Do you adapt your behaviour to suit theirs in order to keep them happy? Trust your gut instinct – if it feels wrong, it probably is!

- Wanting to see you all the time and planning things when they know you already have arrangements with friends/family and sulks when you don't cancel to be with him

- Sulking, glaring, going moody when they don't get their own way

- Being aggressive with others - watch the body language!

- He won't let it drop if you have a difference of opinion – he will go on and on and on about it

- Trying to convince you his ex is to blame for him not seeing his children

- He insists on coming everywhere with you, turns up unexpectedly when he knows you have plans or because he is missing you

- He questions you about your friends/family and criticises them

- He puts you down, calls you names

- He plays mind games - makes negative comments about your appearance

- He makes little comments to let you know he doesn't approve of what you are wearing – 'don't you think that skirt is a bit short', 'you look a bit tarty'

- He dismisses your concerns - he makes you believe it was your fault when he gets angry and lies about things that happened (gaslighting)

- He tries to make you feel sorry for him

- He will try to make you do things you don't want to do - he won't take no for an answer

- He tries to convince you of all the reasons you should be together

- He tries to convince you that you can just be 'friends with benefits'

- He has a sob story about his childhood/previous relationship

- He takes no responsibility for anything - he makes excuses and lies about things

- He exaggerates things and his stories are full of discrepancies

- He quickly assigns himself as a father figure to your children and questions your parenting

- He wants to be number one priority over your children and gets jealous when you spend time with your children

- He favours one child over another

- He chooses your clothes

- He offers to move in with you / get engaged, very quickly

- He takes over everything at home because his way is better and criticises how you do things

- He believes he is better than everyone else

- He wants sex too quickly in the relationship, tries to get you to do things I don't want to and doesn't express affection during sex

- He refuses to wear a condom or share responsibility for contraception

- He only wants sex when he wants it, never any other time

- He has very few or no friends

- He can never keep a steady job — always someone else's fault that he has to leave

- He relies heavily on you for his happiness

- He showers you with affection, gifts and declares undying love after only a couple of weeks (lovebombing)

- He makes excuses not to introduce you to his friends/family

- He takes drugs/drinks heavily

There are lovely people out there — trust me! You just have to filter out the bad ones and this checklist will help you. If it feels wrong, it probably IS wrong.

"Looking back now I can see there were early warning signs, but I just didn't see them at the time. He was always wanting me to be with him, making me feel guilty if I wanted to see my friends, so I would cancel nights out with them. By the time I realised I needed help, I had lost contact with all my friends, so leaving was even harder."

"He was always full of excuses and everything was always about him — every time he lost his job it was always someone else's fault, or he would give it up without a thought about how we might pay the bills. He didn't care how his behaviour affected me as long as he got what he wanted."

CHAPTER 4:

CHILDREN AND CO-PARENTING WITH AN ABUSIVE EX

Children learn from what they see and hear at home – they see much more than you ever want to admit, they hear lots – and actually hearing but not seeing can be scary for them, as their imaginations take hold and they make up their own version of events, but they can recover. This is important to remember. The younger they are when you separate the better, and the sooner they get help to cope with the emotional impact of abuse, the better too. Children don't have to be defined by their experiences either, but if they get specialist support then they will recover much better.

You may notice signs that your children are struggling with the situation at home:

- Clinginess, reluctance to go to school

- Aggressive behaviour at home or in school

- Inability to focus on schoolwork

- Trouble sleeping, nightmares

- Developmental delays

- Poor eating habits

- Inconsolable behaviour

- Soiling themselves or bedwetting

- Getting into antisocial behaviour

- Using drugs/alcohol to cope

Of course, each child is different and the signs also depend on the age of the child. It is important to understand what is normal behaviour for your particular child and recognise when this changes. If your child refuses to go to contact it can be really difficult — highly emotional and distressing for you all, but if you don't abide by the Court Order then you are in breach and there can be consequences to that which your ex will undoubtedly use as ammunition against you.

Your children will have to adapt to different rules and routines in yours and your ex's home and you will have to adapt too. This can be a challenge! You may not want your ex to take your child to certain activities or to contradict your rules and routines. Your ex may try and win favour by buying the children things they know you can't afford or spend lots of time being 'fun dad' while you have to do all the 'boring' things like homework, but there is nothing you can do about it.

Co-parenting with an abusive ex

Abusive relationships are based on power and control. If you end that connection with your ex, they will no doubt try to use the children to keep that connection with you. There are different ways an abusive parent can use the children as another tool to abuse:

The Absent Parent

They may choose to walk away, wanting little or nothing to do with the children. They may be secretive about their new life, they may refuse to pay maintenance or disappear from the children's lives. They may tell you that you won't be able to cope on your own and ignore any attempts from you to co-parent. Unfortunately, in this situation there is little you can do – you can't force someone to be the parent that you want them to be for the children. You may become exhausted trying to do the right thing and offering different options of contact, only to have them ignored or excuses made. This can be difficult for the children to cope with as they may take on misplaced guilt and feel as if it is their fault that the other parent has disappeared from their life.

"My ex turns up as and when he feels like it – he may not appear for a month and then he will turn up and demand to see the children. He won't tell me in advance, saying that he never knows when he is working and he won't tell me where he is taking them. If I try and push for a regular agreement, he threatens me, saying he 'can't be tied down and needs his own space'. I have tried many times to get him to have the children at Christmas and in the school holidays but there is always an excuse as to why he can't have them."

Don't waste time and energy trying to make your ex into the parent you wish he could be. Find some better role models for your children - uncles, friends, group leaders, teachers. There can be many better role models than their actual parent.

The Disguised Compliance Parent

The abusive parent can seem perfectly charming to everyone else – tugging at the heartstrings, claiming that all they want is contact with their children, making everyone feel sorry for them. They may have shown no interest in the children while you were together, but all of a sudden, they want 50/50 contact. Underneath it all, they may be diverting attention away from the facts about their abusive behaviour. They may agree to do parenting programmes, but are they actually attending and putting it into practice or just trying to 'pull the wool over the eyes' of professionals? They may jump on school parent's groups, trying to influence other parents. They will send you endless emails, trying to communicate with you about parenting issues, but only 2 lines of the email will actually be about the parenting issues – the rest will be subtle undermining and criticism of your parenting decisions.

''My ex and I have 50/50 shared care. He constantly pleads on emails to communicate with me face to face, though he knows this is against the court order, but it makes me feel as though I am being unreasonable. He regularly sends messages out to the other parents criticising me as a parent e.g. asking to borrow a school jumper as the one I have sent my daughter in, is too small. It isn't, but he uses this to criticise me to the other school mums and he tries to blame me when I try and keep to the agreement.''

The Aggressive Parent

They will threaten you with and drag you to court at the 'drop of a hat'. They feel completely bereft now that you have left them, they have zero insight into their behaviour and they don't care how it affects you or their children. They are out to win at all costs. They apply for full custody of the children without thought as to whether this would be the best thing for the children or how they would manage that practically and they do this knowing that this will impact future financial payments for the children.

They may make false accusations to distract professionals from everything they aren't complying with and spend the majority of contact trying to quiz the children about you and your life. They either show little interest in the children in between contact visits or try and interfere with your time with the children and they try to buy the children's affection. They tell lies to the children to gain sympathy, they are secretive, they constantly push the boundaries of contact arrangements and spend less effort on creating a new life for themselves and way more time trying to destroy yours.

"My ex took me to court so many times. He used to spend the whole time with the children asking them if I had a new boyfriend, quizzing them about what I was doing now and trying to twist things and turn them against me. One of them had a bad accident when they were with him and he didn't even tell me – I had to find out from the social worker. He takes them on fancy holidays that he knows I can't afford and tells them that they will soon be with him full-time."

Tips for parenting with a controlling ex:

- When they drop off your child in dirty clothes, 'forget' to return your daughter's nicest dress that you sent her in and turn up late, don't rise to the bait. Work around it – send your child in old clothes, clothes you don't mind not getting returned or make sure you have extra sets of clothes at home so you don't get caught short. If the clothes come back smelling of cigarette smoke, don't even mention it to your ex – just get on and wash the clothes.

- If they turn up late on a regular basis, keep a log of it (in case you need evidence for court) but just send your child out, keep conversation very minimal, (ignoring the fact they are late) and act busy or distracted as if you really aren't bothered about the fact that they are late at all. Power crazy ex's will expect you to be ranting at them, wound up and frustrated at their lateness. Throw them a curve ball and do the opposite! Trust me this works! Once they realise this tactic isn't working, they will get bored and stop doing it.

- Keep it 'light and bright' – encourage your child before contact, remind them of the nice/fun things they will be able to do when they get there. Don't let them see you upset – save the tears for when they have gone if you can. Keep it short and sweet – brief conversation with your ex, a cuddle and a kiss for your child, then leave. Ignore any criticisms from your ex, 'paint a smiley face on' and walk away.

- Give your children their favourite toys or activities to keep them busy while with your ex. If your ex is a great parent when the children are with him, great! If he is feeding them junk food and they are complaining about being bored, again, work around it. Feed them before they go or have food ready for when they return. Encourage them and give them ideas on how to keep busy and to amuse themselves while they are there.

- Be prepared for a day or two where your child may feel unsettled. They may feel anxious before contact or afterwards. Encourage them before contact and allow them time to settle afterwards. They will have to get used to different rules in each home, but don't let them manipulate you by playing one parent off against the other.

- If they don't want to go to contact and there is an Order in place, they will have to go, it's as simple as that. If they don't, you will be in Breach and your ex will no doubt be quick to take you back to court. This situation can be extremely difficult, all you can do is try and encourage your child as much as possible, reassure them that they can have a nice time when they are there and give them the reassurance that you will be there afterwards.

- Encourage them to talk about what they are worried about so you can see what you can put in place to reduce their anxiety. Again, keep a log of this and get some support for your child so they have a safe place to offload.

- Give your children guidance on coping strategies they can use during contact. If they are bored, what can they do to amuse themselves? Can they take plenty of toys/books/homework with them? Do they know what to do to manage any feelings of anxiety/anger while they are away from home?

- If they boast about the amazing time they have had with your ex, when you are struggling and perhaps unable to offer them the same experiences, don't get upset or angry about it. Share their excitement at these experiences – yes, your ex may be trying to 'buy' the children's affection, but whatever the reason, your children have been having fun, which is so important and better than them being miserable during contact -and you don't have to pay for it!

- Keep your communication with your ex, brief. Offer up basic information about eating habits, play days, school activities and homework and any health issues.

- You may not get the same amount of information back (again this can be a way they can control things) but don't give them the satisfaction of asking. If you have questions about schooling, ask the teacher, if you have any concerns about your child's health, ask your GP.

- In an ideal world you would be able to have open and honest communication with the other parent but with a controlling ex this is unlikely. Take control, find another way to get this information. If you can't get it, let it go and focus on what is happening when your child is with you instead.

- Children can try and manipulate both parents to their own ends too – they aren't silly! Be consistent with your own rules in your home. Ditch the guilt and parent your children – don't give in to the children's demands because you feel guilty about the upset, children need rules and boundaries.

- Use the time away from your children to do things that are easier to do without them or use the time to build yourself up. Connect with friends, study for a qualification, catch up on work, prepare for court, keep busy – don't waste your time worrying about what they might/might not be doing.

Parental Alienation/Coercive control using the children

Your ex may well try to manipulate the children against you. They may lie to the children, try and convince them that everything is your fault – that you broke up the family, that you are mentally ill, that you are a bully. Any parent that completely tries to annihilate the other is obsessive, determined and if not dealt with quickly can feel empowered and unstoppable. The children will be caught up in the middle and the trauma they can experience can be very difficult (but not impossible) to rectify.

- Get expert help early on if you are concerned about the manipulation of your children. You need expert legal advice if your ex is trying to intent on removing your children from your care. Don't hesitate! The way that your case is handled in the early days can determine the long-term outcomes. If your ex seems determined above all costs to alienate the children against you, you need help.

- If your children seem to be over-reacting to situations, if their reactions seem completely over-dramatic and exaggerated above anything you have seen or heard from them before, if they are using words that you know have come straight out of your ex's mouth, keep a log of it and tell someone. Tell an experienced family solicitor and tell social services as this is emotional abuse.

"My daughter came home from her dad's accusing me of lying throughout her life and about her dad. It was just like listening to him. She was calling me names, telling me I was stupid, bragging about how much money her dad earnt compared to me and she kept arguing with me till the early hours of the morning. It was horrendous and made me feel as if I was back there with him."

- If your children come out with statements that worry you, get them to question those thoughts: "is this what you think? Have you seen me do this? I am not sure that was exactly what happened". This will help them question whether what they have said is a fact or a belief that has been impressed upon them by someone else. If you have evidence that contradicts their beliefs, show them. You can't argue with evidence, but don't get into long, drawn-out conversations about adult issues with them.

- Keep being yourself – show them the real you.

- Keep the boundaries up with them so they don't bully you. Make sure they know there are consequences to abusive behaviour, give them loads of encouragement when they behave nicely or do something well.

- Don't get drawn into the drama. Ignore their accusations or refute them in a calm voice. You don't have to justify yourself to them – explain things briefly and move on.

- It can be so confusing for children who are victims of parental alienation. It is the behaviour you don't love, but you still love them, make sure they know that.

- Get them professional support if you can – they need space to work out their feelings and emotions, to work out how they feel and to manage the internal conflict.

- In situations such as these, you have to be 'over-polite', 'over-accommodating' and 'proactively offering' to support the other parent and the children. The situation has to be black and white. No grey areas. You have to be the saint and he has to be the villain, which sounds awful to say, out loud but you cannot reason with someone who is determined to alienate your children from you.

- They will try and divert attention away from them and towards you. If there are any concerns around the children's behaviour, this has to be apparent during contact with your ex, not you. Everything negative has to happen during his time, not yours. You may understand what is happening here, but professionals may not.

- Stay calm, remove any anger from your communication with your ex. Keep to the facts.

- Think ahead. Be proactive rather than reactive. Their behaviour is very predictable so think of what their next step might be or how they might react and don't fall into their trap.

- Don't compete with your ex. Focus on yourself and your own parenting values, not your ex's. Think of all the positive things you have to offer your children – kindness, honesty, strength, positive role-modelling, security, stability, self-worth.

- Understand your weaknesses. Be honest with yourself and others, don't try to cover them up for fear of them being used against you. If you can be honest it will be much more difficult for your ex to use any faults against you.

- Keep child-focussed. Always be the bigger person and act with kindness. You may win back your children as a result of a court order or when the children grow old enough to work it out for themselves. Stay true to yourself and you WILL win, no matter how long it takes you.

- When you communicate with your ex or professionals, think about the language you use. Instead of saying ''I need contact with my children'', say '' it has been x weeks since the children have had contact with me. How can we move this arrangement forwards? What can you to help the children? What do you suggest?'' Even better, come up with a suggestion of your own that might work.

- Start small and build it up – would it be better to start with a short contact session, perhaps with a 3rd party present? I know this can seem alien and you will be aching for more, but if you suggest something small then this is more likely to be agreed. Better to have some contact than none to start off with.

- Enjoy your life – easier said than done, but children gravitate towards the positives. Show them how you can have fun, build a life outside of your role as a parent.

- Remember you are not alone – you may feel like it as it is difficult for others to understand just how devastating this can be, but you are not. You CAN get through this and you will.

Parenting Agreements

No matter what your ex has done it is highly likely that he will be allowed by any UK court to see their child. You may well be worried about this, but also bear in mind that your child may well want to see them too. If you are worried about your child's safety then you are within your rights to withhold contact, but you must have evidence otherwise you run the risk of being labelled 'obstructive' in Court or even worse being accused of kidnapping your own child.

Rather than thinking of how you can keep your child away from your ex, think about how you can take control and think about how you can make contact work safely and in the best interests of your children.

What days and times might work best for the children? Take into consideration after-school clubs and routines, homework, family time. Think about offering time for contact during the week and alternate weekends – after all, you want some fun time with the children too. Think about sharing birthdays, Mother's/Father's Day, religious festivals and holidays.

Think about how you are both going to communicate with schools – parent's meetings, events, etc. What about bigger decisions, such as when the children have to move schools, how will you decide? What about immunisations, illnesses – how would you like to be advised of any significant health concerns? Who would look after the children if either of you fall ill?

How much notice would you like if the arrangements need to be changed? Keep those boundaries in place as much as possible! What will happen if you have a new relationship? How will you tell the children? How will you tell the children?

Family Court

You have done the one thing your ex never thought you would. You left them. How can they keep control over you now that you are no longer with them? Through the children, that's how. Ex's who never really stepped up as a father when you were together will suddenly want to have full custody of the children. They may initiate proceedings to increase contact, to reduce maintenance or to object to Court orders.

They won't care how it impacts on the children and even less about how it impacts on you. They won't care if it costs them everything – financially or emotionally. This is all about 'the win'. This is about seeking revenge for the fact you left them. This is about them feeling aggrieved, angry, tormented.

You may have no option if your ex starts proceedings against you, but if you do have an option whether to go to Family court or not, think carefully. There is no easy way to say this but the UK Family Court system is broken and unfortunately reform is going to take a long time. There is little recognition of how domestic abuse impacts on the adult victim or the children and a presumption that no matter what, both parents will be able to have contact with their children.

Of course, in an ideal world, all relationship separations would be amicable and children would have contact with both parents equally – both parents would put the children first and bring them up together, communicating politely and nurturing the children, limiting any potential trauma as a result and enabling the children to thrive.

In reality, what I often see if abusers using the court system as another tool to abuse, failing to comply with court orders, using the children as a tool to continue to abuse their victim without any recognition of how this affects their own children and victims feeling unheard, made to feel more vulnerable and faced with ongoing stresses and strains as a result or protracted and expensive court hearings.

However, every case is different, and in some circumstances, going to court CAN give you the protection you need, the consistency and clarity to help you co-parent and the validation of your concerns. It is vital – not just important, but vital, that you get professional help if you want to try and get the best outcomes for you and the children.

"After 4 years and numerous hearings, psychological assessments and more, I was about done - then the final report came in and it was as if he had shot himself in the face, not the foot. He couldn't help himself – blatantly lying, intent on discrediting me, it was all there in black and white for everyone to see. He finally had to accept that contact with him was not in the best interests of the children – they had been traumatised enough and it was going to stop."

Tips for getting through Family Court proceedings:

- Your legal representative needs to have experience of supporting victims of domestic abuse in family court – these cases are not like amicable divorce or separation cases. They are complex, lengthy and extremely challenging.

- You may want to consider signing up to an online court preparation course – they can give you more tips to feel confident about family court. These courses are often run by women who have 'been there and done that' – they are using their experience to help you.

- Many controlling ex's lie to cover up their behaviour and will often come unstuck in court hearings. Evidence is key – stick to the facts, keep your story consistent, allow your team to challenge your ex on the facts and ask for evidence.

"My ex lied so much he forgot what he had said. He supposedly had recordings of me, but then 'lost' his phone and couldn't pro-duce these so-called witnesses he had. It was laughable really, but it made me so angry as he was trying to destroy my family."

- Don't let your ex intimidate you, don't get upset by the lies you might hear and remember this isn't your fault. Hold your head high, look at the judge, not your ex, be honest and tell the truth and 'the truth will out', so the saying goes.

- Keep a log of how the children are before and after contact with your ex, keep any texts or emails from your ex that are threatening, emotionally abusive or harassing, keep evidence of times when your ex hasn't kept to the agreed arrangements and reasons given. Get as much evidence in writing as you can, then it's not just hearsay.

- Don't coach your children on what to say to professionals and don't ask them questions about your ex– this is not appropriate, keep your children out of it. Don't put your children in the middle of the dispute, these are adult problems.

- Keep the interests of the children at the focus of proceedings. This is not about you or your ex or what either of you want, this is about what is in the best interests of the children.

- If you have concerns about the safety of your child in the care of your ex, you need to evidence the reasons why.

- If you have concerns that your ex is using drugs/ alcohol you can request a hair – strand test, preferably one that tests for at least 6 months misuse. If you have concerns about mental health, your Solicitor can request a psychological assessment, but don't sling unfounded accusations at your ex.

- Be prepared to make this work – go in with suggestions for a positive parenting plan. It is highly unlikely that your ex will be prevented from having any contact at all with your children, no matter what has happened in the past, so you need to find a plan that works for you and the children. If you go in with examples of what might work, it shows you are trying, that you have thought about what might work and that you are willing to offer suggestions. Get in their first, take control. You will also have to think about bigger decisions such as the children's involvement in religious festivals, bigger family events, immunisations and school communication.

- How will your communication with your ex take place? Will it be via email, WhatsApp or will you use a parenting App where you can share details about school meals, after-school activities, social invites for your child and finances related to your children?

- You don't have to think about all of these things at once but the more detail you can include in the Child Arrangement Order or the parenting agreement, the less wriggle room there is for your ex to use the contact as a way to manipulate you and the clearer everything is for both parties.

- If you have an agreement about childcare in place make sure you stick to it. There is no point in spending lots of money and energy going through court proceedings to create a plan if neither of you stick to it.

- In an emergency if you believe you child is at risk of harm from abduction, at imminent risk of being taken to another country or you have evidence that your ex is posing significant risk of harm to your child you can go to court to make an emergency application for a Prohibited Steps Order.

Child Maintenance

The abuser may dispute how much maintenance you are entitled to, they may give up work just to ensure that they don't have to pay or they may make you ask them for money for your child, only to refuse you. If they are self-employed, they can be very 'creative' with their finances so that on paper it looks like they hardly earn anything at all. It makes them feel powerful, they don't care if it affects their child, they do it anyway.

If you do go through the Child Maintenance Service they can act as the intermediary. It may take them many months to finalise a regular payment schedule and even then, your ex may continue to avoid paying.

A voluntary agreement with a controlling ex is never a good idea as this provides the perfect means for them to maintain control over you. They may initially agree to give you a set amount each month for your child but lo and behold, when they are in a bad mood or they 'haven't earnt enough that month' or 'just because', they will refuse.

Each time you have to ask your ex for money it leaves you vulnerable - it means you are not in control over your own finances. It may be a bitter pill to swallow but if there are no powers of enforcement regarding maintenance payments, think about how you can manage financially without him.

Take control —financial independence is really powerful. Your ex will no longer have a hold over you. Can you reduce your outgoings and increase your income so you can manage without their money? Can you reduce bigger outgoings like school fees or after-school clubs and sports club fees?

Focus on the bigger picture. You won't have to have those awkward conversations any more with your ex, it cuts down on the amount of communication between you, you don't have to listen to their excuses and you can spend your money however you like because it is absolutely nothing to do with them!

"My ex used to threaten all the time not to pay the school fees. At the time I was desperate to keep the children in that school but I realised if I was ever to be free of him, they had to move. They are now in a local school and loving it. I don't have to worry about fees now and it's one less hold that he has over us."

What if it doesn't go your way

As difficult as it is, accepting that it is better to walk away from conflict with your ex can sometimes be the right thing to do. You know your ex loves a battle – they have determination, they may have the financial wealth to persist with court hearing after endless court hearing, they may be determined above all else to make your life a misery, even for years after you have separated. They thrive on the satisfaction they feel when they see you upset, angry, frustrated and they want to win above all else.

What are you getting out of this? How much is it costing you financially and emotionally? Will the next hearing be the final one or is it likely to continue on and on?

Is there another way to deal with this rather than through court? Sometimes you need to take some time out, to step back and reflect and think about what really matters. Is it absolutely vital that you go to Court again or could you consider re-negotiating so you can actually reach some kind of workable agreement.

How much will it cost you (and more importantly your children) if you disagree? Would it be better to focus your time, money and energy into creating a better life for you and your children rather than fighting another court hearing? Is your ex likely to adhere to any court orders even if you do manage to obtain them?

Consider your motives and potential outcomes at each step. I am not saying 'don't go to court', but just have your eyes open if you do. Family court hearings are rarely simple, they often result in several hearings and can be extremely stressful, as well as financially devastating and extremely time-consuming.

If the court proceedings didn't go your way, it can be devastating. Take some time to just breathe, get over the shock and ensure you have a debrief with your legal team to understand how and why this happened. It may have been due to something completely outside of their control, take time to understand what the options are now and what your next step might be.

Do you want to challenge this outcome? Do you want to seek different legal representation? Are you able to accept the outcome? Can you walk away from court and find a way to work with the current order even though it is not exactly what you wanted?

Remember, court is only one aspect of your life as a parent. You love your child, no matter what your ex says or what the court says. You can continue to build a relationship with your child no matter what happens - it may be in circumstances different to how you imagined, but however it is, you can do it.

When is it time to call time on the battle with your ex? Only you will know that. You will know when you are done. If it is becoming seriously detrimental to your wellbeing, if it is seriously impacting on your mental health, if it is ruining you financially, perhaps it is time. Walking away doesn't mean you don't care. It doesn't mean you are giving up. It doesn't mean you agree with the conditions your ex wants.

What it DOES mean is that you are choosing not to engage with the conflict, that you are choosing to focus on creating a better future for yourself and your family and focussing your energies on that, rather than on feeding your ex's ego.

Use the finances saved on court hearings to buy or rent your new home, to furnish it, to buy yourself a 'break up' holiday to help you recover. Use the emotional energy you are saving to focus on starting a new career, learning and educating yourself on something that will help you in the future. Use the time when you don't have the children with you to do things for you – it will make you happier and ultimately make you a better parent.

"We battled through court for 4 years. It cost me thousands and was causing more and more trauma to my child. Now he has the 50/50 contact order that he wanted so much, he is not bothered! He asks me to have our son more because he has work commitments! My son has learnt how to manage his time at his dad's and his time here. It's not ideal but I am not fighting anymore."

Don't lower yourself to the level of your ex. Let them bask in the glory of you walking away – they will think they have won, but have they really?

" Friends told me that 'what goes around comes around' and it has. My children worked it out for themselves eventually and we started to rebuild our relationship. I will never forgive him for the times I missed with the children but we are closer now and everything is good, so I don't want to be bitter anymore – it's a waste of energy."

Remember – you didn't cause this, you didn't want this, don't let your ex's behaviour ruin your precious time with your children or stop you from recovering. Do what you can to be the best parent you can be, to be the best version of you and never give up hope that things will sort themselves out.

CHAPTER 5:

CREATE A HAPPIER FUTURE

It's as easy as 'ABC'!

It's really important that you consider each of these aspects as you go through the process of separating and building a new life. The legal stuff, the emotional rollercoaster and the hurdles you have to overcome can all lead to overwhelm – feeling like you are never going to get there, like you just don't have the energy to do this anymore. Court proceedings can be all-consuming and leave you little time or energy to focus on anything else, but if you don't, you will end up depressed and exhausted. Court may be important, but it is only one aspect of your life, not all of it. Other parts matter too.

A – Action! The things you need to do to get closer to the life you want to live.

B – Building resilience. Doing the things that help you feel stronger or cope better.

C – Creating a happier future.

It's all about balance. Work on your ABC!

Action

If you can do **an action –** write an email, collate your financial documents, make a call, to help improve your current situation – do it. Each action is a step forwards and it's all progress. Give yourself a small reward when you complete a tough task.

Building resilience

Make sure you factor in time to make yourself stronger. This will help you cope better with the stress of things that are outside your control and will help protect you against depression and overwhelm. Diarise in time to do some meditation, take some time to go for a walk, be around people that lift you up. It's important! Don't think you haven't got time or energy to do these things – they are just as important as your Actions.

Creating a happier future

You need to focus on exactly that – the future. Do your research on where you want to live, start buying items for your new home, sign up to that course you have always wanted to do, create a mood board with pictures and photos of what you want your future to look like. Put it up on your wall to keep you motivated and start taking action to make it happen.

Working on your ABC balances out the negativity. You can't just think about the challenging stuff – you have to feed yourself with a bit of positivity and a bit of calm too if you are going to get through this whole process and stay sane! Remember your ABC and you will feel much better as you navigate this journey.

It takes practice to defend yourself against someone who is so doggedly determined and persuasive and sometimes it seems like they will never leave you alone. You may move on into another relationship – they may even move on and find a new partner, yet here they still are - getting on your nerves, challenging everything you do and every decision you make.

They may appear when you have a wobble - maybe when you are feeling low or lonely and missing some of those special times you had together. When the children are asking to see Daddy and you feel as if you are depriving them of that relationship, when things seem too difficult, you can feel worn down. You let your guard down, you let your boundaries down, giving in to their demands 'just this once' because you are too exhausted for another battle, it can be all too easy to do.

Stop! Before you act, lean on your support team– much better to call them than to call your ex. Call Samaritans, call your domestic abuse worker, your coach, anyone except your ex! Ask them for advice and guidance – what do they think you should do? What do they suggest?

Sometimes you just need another perspective and it all becomes clear and you feel stronger again. Lean on those that can help you when you need it – that's what they are there for and they want to help you. The stronger and more consistent your boundaries are, the stronger you will feel and the quicker you will be able to create a better life for yourself.

Survivor Programmes

Getting support from other people in similar situations to yourself can be empowering – you feel less alone, you are speaking with other people who know what it's like, you gain strength from each other. One such programme is 'The Freedom Programme' – which you can join online, work through individually with a coach or in a group setting. Working through the different tactics of abuse will help you learn how to protect yourself, help you feel more confident about keeping your boundaries up and help you understand how you got here. Probably most importantly of all, it also teaches you the warning signs of abuse so you don't get caught out again!

There are local peer support programmes too – where you don't have to talk about the past. Just having a cup of coffee with someone who can really understand those 'wobbly' days or who can give you a bit of advice about something you are struggling with can really help. Look at your Power and Control wheel too when you are having a wobbly moment. Remind yourself of the ways in which you were controlled, then think about all the things you can do now you're not!

Out with the old, in with the new!

Get rid of reminders of the past. This is a really cathartic thing to do – have a spring clean of everything negative attached to your relationship. You don't have to get rid of everything-not all your memories will be bad or sad. Looking at old photos can be tough. Move the photos into a folder where you can't see them on a daily basis.

Bin the stuff that doesn't bring you happiness any more or that has negative emotions attached to it. The clothes you were made to wear that you actually hated, pictures that your ex bought that you never liked. I binned my wedding bouquet and took great delight in doing so! I knew I should never have married my ex, so binning the flowers was a way to metaphorically bin that marriage for good.

Keep trying new things

I ditched all the clothes I hated wearing – the oversized, frumpy clothes went straight in the bin. I went out and bought some skinny black jeans - there is an upside to prolonged periods of stress, I dropped a dress size! I started wearing brighter lipstick, got my hair cut and pierced my nose! My mum thought I was having a mid-life crisis! You don't have to go that far obviously, but think about what makes YOU feel good.

Clothes are often referred to as your 'suit of armour' and they really do reflect how you feel. If you want to feel more confident in yourself choose colours, materials and shapes that make you feel good. When you go to meetings with your ex or even on handovers, make sure you look great! Show them what they are missing and dress confidently – you will feel fierce! If you don't know how to style yourself any more, get a friend to shop with you, get a makeover, try a new hairstyle. If you get your hair cut shorter and you don't like it, you can always grow it again. It won't be the end of the world, but it might just look amazing!

Experiment, try new things, that way you will find out what you do like and what you don't. These things don't have to cost lots of money either – many make-up counters in department stores offer free makeovers or personal shopping experiences or do a clothes swop with your friends, browse the charity shops for vintage clothing or do a skills swop with someone.

Remember narcissists thrive on seeing you in pain, hurt and lost without them – if you turn up looking smart, confident and full of energy, you can show them what they are missing. Take control and regain the power over your situation whilst looking like a million dollars! Putting on your makeup when you feel nervous or low or giving yourself a spritz with a lovely scent, can really help change your mindset – try it, it works!

"I dyed my hair pink when I left my ex. He always wanted me to hide in a crowd, now I stand out. I wear what I want, when I want and I don't care who does or doesn't like it. It's me, who I am and I love me!"

Change it up

If you always went to the same supermarket to do your shopping together, go to a different one. Try different pubs, gyms, parks to walk in or different routes. These simple strategies stop triggering memories of the past and help you move on. Change your routines - create new ones which allow plenty of time for you to do the things you love.

"We always used to spend every evening watching tv – now I hardly watch it at all. I call friends or do my crochet or write and listen to music. I love that I have all this time now just for me."

Look after yourself

Life with an abuser is exhausting – physically as well as emotionally. You 'walk on eggshells' every day – constantly wondering what mood he is going to be in, what excuse he will come up with to excuse his abusive behaviour, trying to do whatever you can to keep things calm, to make sure he is happy and has no cause at all to shout, scream, hurt.

Leaving an abusive relationship is also exhausting – worrying whether he will turn up at your door, worrying every time your mobile flashes, worrying about finances, housing, the children, the future. It is absolutely vital to a successful recovery that you prioritise looking after yourself. You can't look after others if you don't look after yourself first.

You may feel like curling up in a ball under the duvet all day and that's ok sometimes, but that won't make you feel better in the long run. You aren't a robot, you have feelings, so a good cry and a duvet day occasionally won't do any harm. You need to let out some of the pressure.

Quick Daily tips:

- Set your alarm, get up every day after saying something positive or reading an inspirational quote (you can download Apps for these that send you a quote every day or just google 'inspirational quotes'. Find one that resonates with how you are feeling on a particular day or one that inspires you.

- Go outside for a walk or exercise, even if it is only 10 minutes, it WILL make you feel better and boost those 'happy' hormones. Incorporate a walk into your daily routine – a walk to school rather than taking the car, a walk to the local shop, even just a few minutes of deep breathing while you have your morning coffee outside the back door in the sunshine can all help you cope better.

- If you join a fitness club the others in the group can help keep you motivated too and their positivity can brush off on you. Exercise also gives you an outlet if you are feeling angry and tempted to have a rant at your ex – don't! It won't help - go for a run or do some kind of exercise where you can get rid of all that pent -up emotion instead.

- Look at the leaves on the trees, feel the sunshine on your skin or the rain on your face – mindfulness is a very powerful but simple way to reduce anxiety and stress and help you to feel calm and in control again. It brings you back to the present and reduces those feelings of overwhelm. Take a moment to enjoy the simple pleasures, smells, sounds, without stress.

- Meditation and alternative therapies like Reiki healing, massage, aromatherapy and Pranic healing are great ways to help you feel calmer and less overwhelmed – simple techniques and just a few minutes at the start and end of each day can really help. Alternative therapies are amazing at helping you relax, helping you focus and they really help you manage your stress levels. If you have never tried them, give them a go.

- Focus on enjoying those small moments of joy in each day – the way your children giggle (without you having to keep them quiet), the way you can spend as long as you want in the bath without being criticised, the way you can choose what you want to eat without being told off. Simple pleasures and simple freedoms.

- Treat yourself to a pamper session – wear a new nail colour to add some colour to your day, put a face pack on, have a massage – whatever you choose to do make sure it is for no other reason than because it makes you feel good. Take time to 'indulge' in that process – focus on the colours, the smells, the touch, the feelings – remind yourself of how good it feels to be able to do these things now.

- Use your support team– that's what they are there for – to pick you up when feeling down, to make you feel good about yourself again. They may not always pick up on the fact you need them, so don't hide away, reach out – they will be happy to help you and you might be able to return the favour one day.

- Positive affirmations – I love love, love these! I have them everywhere at home! Put them up where you have the kettle, where you brush your teeth, by your bed, and read them every day. There are millions of quotes on the internet and on Apps these days – they can really change your mindset and remind you of who you are.

Combat the loneliness

Yes, there may be times when you miss them. Remember this is due to the trauma bond. Time is the healer – there is no quick fix. Put the radio or TV on if the sound of silence is too difficult. Sleep in the middle of the bed, so there is no obvious space, make the effort to get out of the house, make the effort to be around other people. Learn to enjoy your own company. If you don't, you run the risk of jumping into another relationship too quickly just to fill that gap.

If you haven't worked on yourself first and got yourself to a place where you feel happy and comfortable with you and the way your life is now, you are likely to attract the wrong type of relationship. You certainly don't want that again, not after all your hard work to be free! Learn to love who you are now. You are enough.

Dating and New Relationships

Yes, it is absolutely possible to find love and have a happy, healthy and fulfilling relationship after domestic abuse. I have been with my husband for over 20 years now – he is my absolute rock - not Mr. Perfect, but who is? He is protective, steadfast, reliable and genuinely one of the most loving and caring people I have ever met – someone who puts everybody else's needs above his own.

Don't jump from one bad relationship into another bad relationship – learn the tactics of abuse, understand them and digest them until you can recount the names of each tactic without even thinking. By doing this you will be able to protect yourself from abuse in future – this is a very empowering feeling.

"My friends told me I wasn't allowed to choose any more partners as I kept getting it wrong! Now I know I can, because I can spot the tactics straight away."

Just give yourself a breather. Spend time alone – learn to enjoy your own company, spend time enjoying things you choose, without having to consider anyone else. You have put someone else's needs way above your own for a long time now, so now it's time for you to just think about you. If you get into another relationship you won't get that 'me' time again – well not as much of it, so make the most of it now. Relish in the selfishness of just thinking about yourself.

Be happy with yourself and your life before you let someone else into it again. Regain some of your confidence, do some work on understanding what your own values are, learn from your previous relationship and understand your boundaries. This preparation work will ensure that you are clear on what you want from your next partner.

What things have you learnt from this relationship that you can take to the next one? Are there things you definitely wouldn't put up with next time?

Final words

Don't let anyone tell you that abuse was your fault. Friends and family may never understand your experiences, let it go. Don't listen to the people that try to hold you back, that try to silence your voice. Don't seek validation from the person that abused you – who needs to listen to their opinions and ideas about your worth? As long as you know what your worth is, that is all that matters!

Everyone has a fire inside of them that drives them towards bigger and better things. Sometimes we achieve our goals because we are nurtured, encouraged and supported. Sometimes it is because we have no option – sink or swim!

These strategies take practice. You can't just do them once and expect your life to change overnight. If you have children with your ex you are likely to have to deal with them for many years to come. You will become more resilient, less affected by their behaviour but you will need to use all of these techniques to help you. They are not about to have a 'personality transplant' so you had better know how to deal with them, life is too short!

The only person that has ultimate control over your life is you. Practice, practice, practice these strategies on a daily basis until they become second nature to you. There is no magic wand to wave - you ARE the magic wand.

If you work on all of these strategies, bit by bit a new, happier life will fall into place. There may be hurdles, there may be the odd setback, you will have to make some tough choices along the way, but you will able to deal with them. You won't take crap from anyone! You won't let things get you down.

Embracing this new mindset is so empowering - I can't fully describe just how good it feels, you have to try it for yourself!

"I said on my 10th wedding anniversary: Do you still want to be in this situation in another 10 years – I didn't."

"The first step is the hardest thing you will ever do, but it's so worth it. Never look back. No matter how small the steps, keep going. Believe in yourself and love yourself first."

"Fear of the unknown can keep us in a toxic relationship. The longer you are paralysed by fear, the more you sacrifice your chance of happiness. There comes a point when you have to say no more."

"At times getting to the finishing line seemed impossible to me, but I visualised a life of being "normal" - such as not being scared anymore, smiling and laughing again and being independent in all areas of my life. I wanted my daughter to have a good role model of what it's like to live life your own way and have dreams and opportunities again. "

Domestic abuse shapes you, but it isn't YOU. Forgive yourself for past mistakes made as a result of the abuse – you did the best you could with the knowledge and the resources you had at the time. Remind yourself from time to time of just how far you have come. You can survive. You can thrive. You can embrace a braver, more confident, more competent and happier YOU. You can do it!

There is help available.

You are not alone.

This is not 'The End', it's just the beginning!

Relationship Balance Tool

WHAT IS YOUR RELATIONSHIP BASED ON?

IS IT EQUALITY?	OR POWER & CONTROL?
Non -Threatening Behaviour Talking & acting to help you feel safe and comfortable, able to express yourself	**Intimidation** Making you afraid by using looks, actions & gestures Smashing things Destroying your property Abusing pets Displaying weapons
Respect Listening to you non-judgementally, affirming, understanding & valuing your opinion	**Emotional Abuse** Putting you down Making you feel bad about yourself Calling you names Making you think you are crazy Playing mind games Humiliating you Making you feel guilty
Trust & support Supporting your goals in life, respecting your right to your own feelings, friends, activities, and opinions	**Isolation** Controlling what you do, who you see & talk to, what you read & where you go. Limiting your outside involvement Using jealousy & love to justify their actions
Honesty & Accountability Accepting responsibility for themselves. Acknowledging past use of violence, communicating openly and truthfully. Admitting when wrong	**Minimizing, Denying, Blaming** Making light of the abuse & not taking your concerns about it seriously Saying the abuse didn't happen Shifting responsibility for their abusive behaviour – saying you caused it
Responsible Parenting Sharing parental responsibilities Being a positive Non-violent role model for the children	**Using Children** Making you feel guilty about the children Using the children to relay messages Using parental Rights to harass you Threatening to take the children away
Shared Responsibility Mutually agreeing a fair distribution of work Making family decisions together	**Economic Abuse** Preventing you from getting or keeping a job Making you ask for money Giving you an allowance Taking your money Not letting you know about or have access to family income
Economic Partnership Making money decisions together Making sure both partners Benefit from the arrangements	**Male Privilege** Treating you like a servant Making all the big decisions Acting like the "King of the Castle" Being the one to define men's & women's roles
Negotiation & Fairness Seeking mutually satisfying resolutions to conflict Being willing to compromise Accepting change	**Coercion & Threats** Making or carrying out threats to hurt you Threatening to leave you Threatening to commit suicide or report you to Social Services Making you withdraw from criminal proceedings Making you do things you wouldn't usually agree to

Happy Couples Checklist

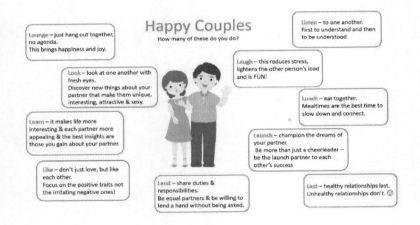

Happy Couples
How many of these do you do?

Lounge – just hang out together, no agenda.
This brings happiness and joy.

Look – look at one another with fresh eyes.
Discover new things about your partner that make them unique, interesting, attractive & sexy.

Learn – it makes life more interesting & each partner more appealing & the best insights are those you gain about your partner.

Like – don't just love, but like each other.
Focus on the positive traits not the irritating negative ones!

Lend – share duties & responsibilities.
Be equal partners & be willing to lend a hand without being asked.

Listen – to one another.
First to understand and then to be understood.

Laugh – this reduces stress, lightens the other person's load and is FUN!

Lunch – eat together.
Mealtimes are the best time to slow down and connect.

Launch – champion the dreams of your partner.
Be more than just a cheerleader – be the launch partner to each other's success

Last – healthy relationships last.
Unhealthy relationships don't. 😞

Sources of Help

National Domestic Abuse Helpline: 0808 2000 247 freephone 24 hours a day

Women's Aid: www.womensaid.org.uk

Refuge.Org: www.refuge.org.uk

Respect.Org: www.respect.uk.net for advice and support with abusive behaviour

Galop LGBT+/Domestic Abuse Helpline: 0800 999 5428

Karma Nirvana Helpline: 0800 5999 247 for Honour Based Abuse

Surviving Economic Abuse: www.survivingeconomicabuse

Rights of Women: www.rightsofwomen.org.uk for guidance on legal process

The Dash Charity: www.thedashcharity.org.uk for domestic abuse support in Royal Borough of Windsor & Maidenhead or South Buckinghamshire

Saneline: www.saneline.org.uk Tel: 0300 304 7000

Samaritans: www.samaritans.org Tel: 116 123 freephone

The Group Hug: www.thegrouphug.com for advice and online support

Glossary

Lovebombing: When the abuser bombards you with love, undying affection and promises to make you believe that this is 'true love'. Your guard drops and this makes it harder to leave when you do recognise abusive behaviour.

Trauma Bonding: A psychological response to abuse. Powerful feelings that you struggle to control and make sense of when your abuser is cruel and kind to you.

Gaslighting: A form of psychological abuse that makes you question your own sanity, memories and recollection of events. Abusers will lie about events, may accuse you of being mentally ill and make you doubt yourself.

Walking on eggshells: The nervous feeling you get when you are constantly trying to keep things calm and worry about what might trigger another incident of abuse.

Lightbulb moment: The moment when you disconnect from your abuser emotionally. You recognise what has been happening and you are ready to do something about it.

PTSD: Post Traumatic Stress Disorder: A broad term to describe symptoms triggered by abuse that can impact on daily life even when you know you are safe. This can include panic attacks, difficulty sleeping, flashbacks

Flashbacks: Vivid experiences where you relive a snapshot of a past experience or event as if it is happening in the present.

IDVA: Independent Domestic Violence Advocate. The specialist workers trained in supporting victims of domestic abuse. They are often based within local domestic abuse organisations but may also be situated in other places such as police stations, hospitals, housing teams and courts.

Refuge: A place of safety you can go to if you feel too unsafe to stay in your home area. These are usually for women and children but there are some specifically for men, older women and for women with language and cultural needs in the UK.

Grounding techniques: Used to describe simple techniques to relieve overwhelm and anxiety. When you feel you are starting to panic, you can use breathing and mindfulness techniques to calm and relive the symptoms.

Cut the cord: Detach yourself emotionally from your abuser. Whatever they do, don't fall for it. Stay focussed on you, rather than on them.

Brave the wave: Imagine the abuser's words as a huge wave washing right over the top of you without soaking into your skin. Don't believe what they say, don't react to it, stay calm and let the words wash over you. Visualise the words creating a puddle on the floor, drying up in the sun – gone forever.

Bin the past: Get rid of anything related to your relationship that holds negative emotions – photos, things in your home, clothes. Only have things in your home that make you feel happy.

Puncture your stress bucket: Do things that help you cope better and feel stronger. This will make it easier to cope with the stress of other things. Don't let your stress bucket overflow (overwhelm).

Stuffing your emotions: Pretending that you are doing ok by avoiding the issue. This does you no good in the long run. Face your fears head on and take control.

Gratitude list: A list or a picture of everything you have in your life to feel grateful for. When you start to focus on this, you balance out the stress and negativity elsewhere.

Limiting beliefs: The doubts you have about your capability because of what you have been told by your abuser. These are not the truths, but are said time and time again to destroy your confidence and prevent you from leaving.

Triggers: Anything that provokes a memory of an abusive experience. These can be sounds, places, experiences, noises, etc. that trigger upsetting or anxious emotions.

Parental alienation: A term used to describe when children become estranged from the other parent as the result of psychological manipulation. Parental alienation is a process of one parent (known as the alienating parent) influencing a child to turn against and reject their other parent (known as the targeted parent) without legitimate justification. The abusive parent may involve other agencies such as social services and courts and make false allegations to distract attention from their own abusive behaviour.

Remember your ABC:

A is for Action – do at least one action to make progress with your current situation.

B is for Build resilience – do the things that make you feel stronger and cope better.

C is for Create a happier future – set some goals and take some steps towards creating a happier future.

Affirmations: short, positive quotes that change your mindset. They remind you of your strengths, your capabilities and give you motivation and encouragement to keep going.

ABOUT THE AUTHOR

Caron understands what it is like to 'walk on eggshells', to feel trapped in an abusive marriage, to be locked in conflict with a controlling ex. Caron lost everything when she left her abuser – she was homeless, she'd lost her child, she was in debt and emotionally broken.

Caron knew that something had to change. If her ex wasn't going to change, she had to. With a successful career in the NHS, Caron decided to use her personal experience to help others and volunteered at her local domestic abuse organisation.

Within a week, she had asked them for a job. That was 14 years ago and Caron has worked passionately in the domestic abuse sector ever since. Caron trained as one of the first Independent Domestic Violence Advocates (IDVA's) in the UK and has worked in various frontline and leadership roles in the domestic abuse sector, supporting hundreds of women.

Caron was the winner of 'Charity Comms' Inspirational Speaker of the Year in 2014 for her work training professionals to respond better to victims of domestic abuse, and she admits she can talk about domestic abuse 'until the cows come home'! Caron now combines her work with The Dash Charity, with her private work supporting clients all over the UK as a Divorce Coach, specialising in abusive relationships.

Caron lives in Buckinghamshire, is happily re-married with 3 grown-up children and now makes time to enjoy the simple pleasures in life - holidays with her family, running, and the odd glass of gin.

🌐 www.caronkippingcoaching.com

in www.linkedin.com/in/caron-kipping//

@CaronKippingCoaching

@caronkippingcoaching

@caronkipping

Printed in Great Britain
by Amazon